Welcome
to English Network Conversation

To help you understand the basic ideas behind **English Network Conversation** I would like to answer four questions.

Is English Network Conversation the right course for me?

I expect you have already studied English for several years. You might have attended a *Volkshochschul-* or some other English course which has helped you to become fairly fluent in English. Most probably, though, you still feel the need to improve your vocabulary, to become more certain in using the right tenses and structures and to react more spontaneously when choosing the right phrases. You may have reached the level of the European Language Certificate in English, Stage 2 (also known as *Volkshochschul*-Certificate) and would like to participate in a conversation course that is a little more ambitious. Or you might be just above the intermediate level and would like to face the challenge of new materials and create more lively discussions corresponding to your interests.

How will English Network Conversation cater for my personal needs?

English Network Conversation will help you to become a more confident speaker of English. It offers ample opportunities not only to talk, but also to read, listen and sometimes to write about topics of general interest and about matters you might feel concerned about. The tasks and various approaches to the texts are thought-provoking and motivating, inviting every individual learner of the group to participate as often as possible. Your personal contribution, therefore, your ideas, experience and feelings are as relevant as the book itself. And your teacher can support you in creating a positive and encouraging atmosphere where you feel ready to co-operate, share and help everybody else enjoy the progress you will experience in your discussions and in your knowledge of English.

What is so special about English Network Conversation?

English Network Conversation is clearly structured, but at the same time it leaves space for flexibility. There are six main topics, which consist of two units each. The two units are united under the same theme but they often present contrasting features. Each unit is set on a double page and depending on how deeply your group gets involved in the subject or the tasks, one unit might cover one to two 90-minute lessons. But as each individual page offers a 'warmer' leading into the subject dealt with, you are welcome to work on one page at a time. Although **English Network Conversation** provides variety, choice and a number of creative inputs, this well-organised double-page system leaves you and your teacher the freedom to add any article or visual material which might support the discussion. You may even decide on a different order for the six topics.

Apart from the shorter texts in the units, **English Network Conversation** introduces you to longer stories or literary extracts. There are six **Activity reading** sections, each relating to one of the six main topics. The aim of these pages is not necessarily for you to read the story during the lesson but to get involved in the speculative predictions which motivate you to read it at home. Facts on some of the authors, or on other aspects of general interest, can be found under the heading **Cultural information** at the back of the book.

Will English Network Conversation help me to improve my accuracy?

You might not want to be reminded of the word 'grammar' in a conversation course, but you probably still feel the need to practise accuracy as much as fluency. The page **Language in action** which appears at the end of each topic holds the answer to this problem. During this 90-minute lesson you will mainly be talking, but you will be concerned with structures rather than topics. And you will have fun with grammar as well. In addition to this, there are six **Selfstudy** double pages and a **Grammar** section at the back of the book to help you consolidate your knowledge independently.

The alphabetical English-German **Dictionary** supports you when in need of an unknown word. This wordlist is no substitute for a real dictionary, though, not even a small one. Therefore, the **Dictionary skills** give you some ideas on how to use a monolingual dictionary. And last but not least we provide you with some helpful tips on what you can find on the **Internet**.

I hope you enjoy your lessons and discussions as much as I enjoyed the writing of this book.

Silvia Stephan

Contents

🔊 = Text on CD 📚 = Activity reading
✏️ = Selfstudy **G** = Grammar

Contents

Topic 1

Satisfying our needs

What do the four pictures have in common?
Choose one picture which
a) expresses 'Moments of happiness' best,
b) represents 'My best investment' most convincingly.

Unit 1 Moments of happiness

1 Tune in

Choose one of these expressions and try to think of a situation where you felt exactly this way. Sit in small groups and tell each other about it.

- I felt happy.
- I was delighted.
- I felt hopeful.
- I felt very pleased.
- I felt ecstatic.
- I was basically content.
- I was very moved.
- I felt great.
- I felt relieved.
- I was overjoyed.
- I almost burst with pride.
- I felt deeply stirred.

2 Read and find out

Five people of different age groups talk about their moments of happiness. Read the texts and match the following names and photos with them. Work with a partner and give reasons.

Tom – nearly 12

Roy, 67 – a retired engineer

Yvette, 22 – a student

Julia, 47 – a teacher

Rodney, 53 – a chauffeur

1

My mood has so much to do with the weather. A beautiful sparkling day makes my spirit soar. I get a great surge of well-being. Then going on holiday, knowing we're off, I get the same butterflies of excitement I got as a child. The kindness of strangers can be very moving. They can make you feel a bit more hopeful about being human.

2

In my first few days at college I felt ecstatic because I was independent for the first time. I had been aiming to go to university for so long, it was a relief. And then, when I finally passed my practical driving test last month, I was overjoyed. I passed the theory a week later. It felt as if I had been learning for ever, and I was delighted.

3

I always feel happy just before I go on holiday or if I've got something I've really wanted for a long time. Probably the last time I felt really, really happy was when I was allowed to take some money out of my bank account to buy a skateboard. I felt great when I got the board. It was expensive but worth it. I was very pleased with myself.

4

When I first saw my new grand-daughter, I felt the purest love. I didn't see very much of my own children when they were growing up, and I regret that now, because I can watch Sarah and see what I missed. I suppose I was always so busy working. The idea of retirement horrified me. Yet I would say I am as happy now as I have ever been.

5

My schooldays were the happiest of my life. I have rarely felt the same happiness since. Nowadays, I am basically content, but I rarely have the same highs. In my twenties I felt deeply stirred by my first sight of the Grand Canyon. I just stood there for ages enjoying this exquisite sense of pure joy. It was almost like being drunk.

3 Share your ideas

Do any of these stories remind you of an experience where you felt almost the same?
Discuss in small groups and report to the class later, if you like.

4 Put meaning into words

Find more phrases used in the texts to express positive feelings.
Then look at task 1 again and make a list of words and phrases you would use to express negative feelings, for example: *felt unhappy, felt displeased*. Use your dictionary.

5 Exchange information

Which of these questions do you find most relevant to talk about? Exchange your ideas with a partner. If you like, ask your teacher.

1 Do you like your work?
2 What do you dislike about it?
3 What is important to you?
4 What do you sometimes miss in everyday life?
5 How do you keep yourself in a good mood?
6 What does happiness mean to you?

6 Read and use these expressions

Sit in small groups and read the text. After every passage make assumptions based on what you have read. Use the expressions that appear after each paragraph. Then compare your points of view in class.

The *singing* **conductor**

Baysee Rowe, 29, is a London bus conductor on the number 38 route, which runs from Victoria to Clapton Pond. He has been singing to his passengers for a number of years. His first single, Sugar Sugar, released on his own label, Double Decker, reached No 30 in the UK and No 1 in South Africa. He has four children, from five months to 11 years old, all of whom live with their mothers. He lives on his own in Leyton, east London.

We suppose/assume that ...

He doesn't have much of a social life any more, but he doesn't get lonely. "With music you are never alone," he says. "Music is the best wife you could have, she never argues and she always pleases." He would like to be married but it just hasn't happened. All women want attention and he hasn't got that kind of time.

We have the feeling that ...

His flat is basically a recording studio. He has £15,000 worth of recording equipment – he bought it piece by piece – but he doesn't own a washing machine or a bed. It doesn't bother him. He is a late sleeper. He just drags the sofa cushions onto the floor and throws a duvet over himself.

We imagine him to ...

He isn't too bothered about food either. He thinks that musicians are terrible eaters because they just don't have the time. He spends the majority of his spare time composing. He writes down an idea on the back of a ticket, then comes home and puts it down on tape.

He seems (doesn't seem) to ...

7 🔊 Listen and answer

Baysee talks about his regular work and the people he meets on the bus. Can you answer the questions listed in task 5 as if you were him? Sometimes, neither the text, nor what he says, gives you a definite answer, but try to imagine what his answers might be like. Sit in small groups and take some notes. Then compare your ideas.

8 Discuss

Do you know anybody like Baysee who can easily make people feel happy?

Unit 2 My best investment

1 Tune in

There are many kinds of investments and a lot of different ideas about what, where, why and how to invest. What do you personally associate with the word 'investment'? Add some words and share your ideas.

Investment

money

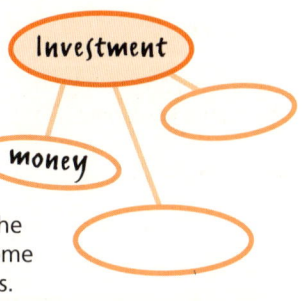

2 Exchange information

Discuss your answers to these questions with a partner. Are your experiences similar?
1 What do you consider to be your best investment?
2 Did you have to put a lot of money or effort into it?
3 In what way has it been rewarding for you?
4 What kind of satisfaction did you, or do you still, get in return?

3 Read and use these expressions

Read the statements 1-8 from below and tick the ones which you personally find relevant. Then compare in small groups and give reasons for your choice. Use these expressions.

To start with, ...   In addition, ...
And another thing, ...   And besides, ...
Not only that, but ...

1 ☐ My patience has been a marvellous long-term investment.
2 ☐ I have invested a lot of effort and hard work.
3 ☐ Good fashion is definitely worth investing in.
4 ☐ I've never felt a desire for wealth or for seeking out investments.
5 ☐ I suppose my best investment has been – and still is – my job.

6 ☐ I've never been a great believer in investing in shares.
7 ☐ My house is obviously my best financial investment.
8 ☐ I've always been looking for precious things, like jewellery and art.

4 🔊 Listen and make your choice

Although Patricia (P), Steve (S), Joanne (J) and Ronald (R) are all fairly well-off, their investments are not always judged in financial terms. Listen to them talking about what they regard as their best investment. After each part, write P, S, J or R next to two of the eight statements above that most closely reflect the opinion of the person speaking. At the end, compare your choice. After listening for a second time, answer the questions in task 2 for each person.

5 Share your ideas

Which of the four people from task 4 would you like to spend an evening with? Discuss in small groups, considering the expressions listed above in order to add reasons.

6 Discuss and write

You have just found this advertisement in a newspaper. In small groups, add two more questions to the ones given on the right. Then compare.

1 How important is money for children?
2 How can parents teach their children about the value of money?

Children's Money Management Camp

a financial course for kids

The best investment for your child

- Every child needs as much help as possible to make it in the job market.
- Your children have credit cards and bank accounts – they need to be taught to manage money.
- They can learn how to be wealthy – how to take risks – We'll take care!
- Five mornings of investment and insider trading – and five afternoons of ice-cream by the swimming-pool.

Here's what a 12-year-old says:
"Since I have been coming to the money camp, I have learnt to take a risk. I'm the owner of 7.500 Canadian oil shares, bought for 32p each and now worth £2.60 each. If I start putting my money to work now, I will make far more from it than if I start at 40."

The Breakers Money Management Camp can be contacted on 00-1-561-655 6611

---

7 Read and put meaning into words

With a partner, fill the gaps in the text with these adverbs:

additionally, carefully, certainly, completely, confidently, exceptionally, ~~expensively~~, hard, seriously.

I want to be a millionaire

A Ron lives in Ascot, England. He is being ___expensively___ educated. He knows the seat and row number on his favourite transatlantic airline from London to Miami. Walking _____ through the imposing corridors of the Breaker Hotel in Palm Beach, Florida's home for the old-moneyed and filthy rich, Ron looks _____ at home. He could be any global investment big-hitter on holiday. However, Ron is only 12 years old and he is at the world's children's Money Management Camp to learn how to be wealthy. While most 12-year-olds worry about whether they are wearing the latest Nike trainers, Ron _____ saves his money. He doesn't tell the other guys at school that he has investments or that he goes to the camp, though. They wouldn't understand. He just wants to learn to manage money and try _____ to succeed one day.

B In the hope of preparing their offspring for the minefields of money management, parents from California to Kansas dig deep to find the £500 to pay for five mornings of investment and insider trading and five afternoons of ice-cream by the swimming-pool or croquet on the hotel's beautiful lawns. The Breakers' _____ luxurious rooms cost extra, as does Ron's favourite seat, 16C on American Airlines. His father _____ believes that children should not only have some kind of financial education at school, but should _____ be taught what it costs to go to college, to buy a house, those sorts of things. If they start putting their money to work now, they will _____ make far more from it than if they start at 40.

---

8 Make your point

Express your reaction to the text by ticking any of the following statements. Then compare in small groups and give reasons.
- ☐ It makes me laugh.
- ☐ It makes me feel angry or upset.
- ☐ I can't believe it.
- ☐ It makes me think of something in particular.

9 Discuss and use these expressions

Work in two groups. Group A describes Ron and group B talks about Ron's father. Take notes and compare in class later. Use these expressions.

He seems to be ...   He probably ...
Presumably he ...   It looks as if (he) ...

Language in action

1 Make your choice

These adjectives can express positive or negative feelings or status of mind:

🙂 all right, at ease, comfortable, encouraged, fine, motivated, perfectly happy, pleased, satisfied

🙁 aggressive, annoyed, anxious, ashamed, awkward, discouraged, displeased, embarrassed, frustrated, furious, irritated, nervous, strange, stupid, uncomfortable, worried

Can you add more words to these lists?

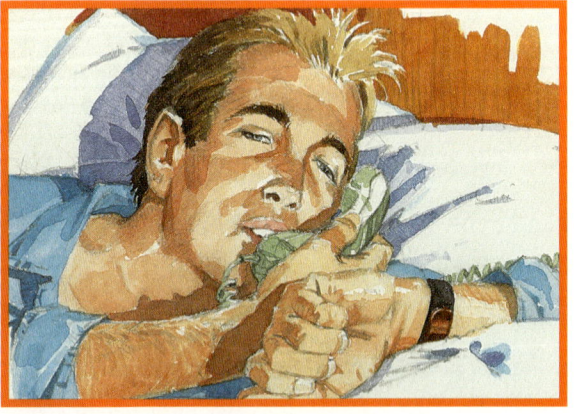

Now express your feelings considering the following situations. Use the adjectives above.

1 I feel .... when somebody rings me in the middle of the night.

2 I feel .... when people are unfriendly.

3 I feel .... when a stranger asks me something on the street.

4 I feel .... when I can't remember something.

5 I feel .... when people are late.

6 I feel .... when somebody interrupts me while I'm working.

7 I feel .... when people don't listen to what I'm saying.

8 I feel .... when I can't find the right words in English.

9 I feel .... when I'm corrected in class.

10 I feel .... when I try to imitate native pronunciation.

2 Read and react

Work with a partner and read six of the following statements each, expressing the appropriate mood as well as possible.

1 You always make me wait for at least half an hour. (*annoyed*)

2 I've been looking forward to this holiday for so long and now I can't go. (*disappointed*)

3 You know what? I'm going to get married next month. (*happy*)

4 Oh dear, I didn't know anything about it. (*surprised*)

5 I'm so glad to hear that you've passed the test. (*pleased*)

6 It's too late now. I can't finish it, I'm afraid. (*tired*)

7 Well, thank you so much for everything. (*friendly*)

8 Peter has invited me for dinner. Isn't that wonderful? (*excited*)

9 That sounds great. Tell me more about it. (*interested*)

10 He hasn't come home yet. I wonder where he is. (*worried*)

11 Oh, what a mess! Can't you ever keep things in order! (*annoyed*)

12 What a wonderful party! Don't you think so? (*delighted*)

3 Write and play your role

Choose one statement from task 2 and write a dialogue of about six lines, adding any phrase before or after the sentence given. Perform your dialogue.

4 Put meanings into words

Write four sentences about yourself, using any of the adverbs below. Then, exchange your notes with a partner and ask each other questions on what you've written, for example:

– *I know France relatively well.*
– *How often have you been there?*
– *How do you usually travel?*

absolutely, completely, considerably, enormously, exceptionally, extremely, incredibly, particularly, perfectly, reasonably, relatively, terribly, undoubtedly.

5 Write and share your ideas

In small groups, write down questions you would like to ask one of the people in the pictures above. Then, exchange notes with another group and discuss some possible answers.

● Have you ever ... ?
● Have you ... a lot during your life?
● Have you ... since you left school?
● Have you ... recently?

Topic 2

Setting priorities

Unit 3 **Personal values**
Unit 4 **Personal achievements**

What kind of things do you imagine each of these four people regard as very important?

What are your priorities in everyday life?

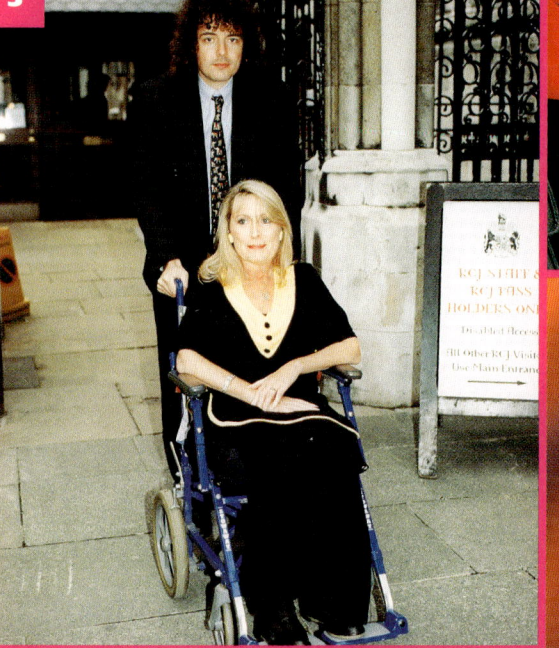

Unit 3 Personal values

1 Tune in
Which of the headlines on the right attracts your attention most? Decide what the article might be about and why you would most likely want to read it. Talk to a partner.

① **True nature of selfishness**

④ **Learning a new quality: Patience**

② **Key to better reading**

③ **The most precious job**

⑤ **Second-class citizens**

2 Read and find out
Match the headlines with the four extracts. Which article is missing? Which one do you think the picture could refer to? In groups of three, write one headline that covers all four articles. Share your ideas.

A I have felt angry for a long time that women who stay at home to look after their children are made to feel like second-class citizens. Looking after children properly is a full-time job. If more women put the welfare of their children first instead of holidays, second cars and luxuries for the home, we might not have so many disturbed youngsters roaming our streets and even committing crimes.

B I don't agree that the 48-year-old mother-to-be has been selfish in putting her career and the making of money before both marriage and children. How many thousands of men do this regularly? Some women do not feel maternal until later in life, just as some men do not feel paternal.

C Children whose mothers go out to work have been found to score higher in reading tests. The best readers at seven are those whose mothers began working from the time they started nursery school. Working mothers tend to be organised and make time for reading with their children.

D Women who do not have paid jobs outside the house devote about 71 hours a week to their domestic work. But the most precious wife – one with a child under a year old – is worth more, about the salary a production manager would earn. A woman with a full-time job spends more time working in the home than at her official place of employment.

3 Discuss and write
The authors of the four articles are a teacher (A), a student (B), a psychologist (C) and a journalist (D). Work in four groups, group A, B, C and D. Write one or two additional sentences to your article and decide what kind of picture you would like to have with it in a newspaper.

4 🔊 Listen and make your choice
You're going to hear a conversation between the authors of the extracts above. There are six statements. Match each of them with one of the articles A (2x), B, C (2x) or D. While listening a second time, pay attention to the way the speakers express agreement or disagreement. Take notes. Do you agree with their opinions?

5 Put meaning into words

With a partner, decide which of the words below might belong together. Don't look at the text. What do the word-pairs tell you about someone's life? Discuss in small groups.

1 neat and	5 stifling	9 it became
2 rebellious	6 feel	10 golden
3 family	7 endless	11 a look of
4 fond	8 wrong	12 second

- ☐ a) opportunity
- ☐ b) embarrassed
- ☐ c) hard work
- [11] d) disgust
- ☐ e) chance
- ☐ f) essential
- ☐ g) children
- ☐ h) tidy
- ☐ i) memories
- ☐ j) direction
- ☐ k) problems
- ☐ l) room

6 Read and make your point

Underline all the statements which you personally agree with or which are true for you. Then, share your ideas with a partner.

OBSESSED BY A NEED TO LEARN
Jane was never enamoured of school – until she had a second chance

When I was at school, everybody would say to me "School days are the best days of your life." I would look at them in horror. If these days are the best, what must it be like to be a fully-fledged adult? No wonder they all look so worried and tired!

Now that I'm a fully-fledged grown-up myself, I look back on my school days with fond memories. I even hear myself talking about it to my own children and see them staring back with that same look of disgust I once perfected. Oh yes, I clearly remember sitting exams. I used to think they were the equivalent of a death sentence. First the revision, hours of endless hard work. Then the exam where we were made to sit in a stifling room with nothing but a pen and a piece of paper. I was one of those many re-bellious children who just couldn't be forced to sit down and learn. Now when I reflect, I feel embarras-sed and I regret not having been more ambitious. I don't really know when the change occurred. One moment I didn't care and the next I was obsessed. The need to learn became essential. I began to picture myself back at school with a new pen and a clean exercise book with

that perfectly blank first page which was always so neat and tidy. I suddenly felt the need to know, the need to do something more challenging, the need to learn. And I finally decided to complete a ten-week 'return to learning' course.

For many teenagers, school years can be traumatic. They have to overcome family problems as well as trying to study for exams. Let the youngsters do their best, but to push them in the wrong direction can often be a push over the edge. Let them have a few years travelling around the world. What better way to learn about the Sphinx, Niagara Falls, volcanoes, mountains, cultures, languages and, most of all, about people? My son was given an atlas for his sixth birthday. I love it. I have learnt more from that little atlas than I ever did when I was studying for my geography exams. So far I've travelled quite a bit in Europe so I could relate to the places I visited and I could shout in excitement, "Yes, I know, I've been there!".

So for me, a second chance at education became a golden oppor-tunity. In order to learn, you must want to. In my opinion, the best time to learn is after 22 and I don't regret having had my family first. Then, at least, you have a vague idea of what you might like to do with the rest of your life. After all, the average person lives to the ripe old age of 80 nowadays. You don't need to rush for the sake of five years.

7 Discuss and use these expressions

Do you completely agree with Jane's opinion or do you have certain reservations? What do you disagree with? Discuss in small groups first and then in class. Use these phrases.

In my opinion, ...
I personally think/feel that ...

I agree completely.
I think so, too.
You may be right.

I see your point, but ...
I don't quite agree with you.
I'm afraid, I disagree entirely.

Unit 4   Personal achievements

1 Tune in

Copy two out of these six questions onto a piece of paper. Then, get up and interview at least three partners. Write down their names and answers. Finally, report to the class.

1 What memories do you have of your school days?
2 Where did you learn what is useful to you now?
3 What does success mean to you?
4 Which personal achievement are you particularly proud of?
5 What are you fairly good at?
6 Is there anything which you would still like to achieve or learn?

2 Discuss and use these expressions

In small groups, choose one of the four people in the pictures of page 13. Which two questions would you ask this person? Answer them in his/her name. Finally, report to the class giving reasons for your choice and expressing uncertainty in what you know. Use these expressions.

We don't know for certain, but we think ...
We may be wrong, but ...
We have the feeling that ...
We couldn't really say for sure, but ...

3 ◄)) Listen and answer

You are going to hear a radio interview with a young and successful executive, Mr James Lewis. During the programme, people are invited to ask the young man any questions they like, some of which are listed in 'Tune in'. After listening to the text, answer these questions for James. Speculate in small groups, using the expressions from task 2 again.

4 ◄)) Listen and write

While listening a second time, try to complete these phrase openings by adding one or two words. Then compare and add anything missing with the help of a partner.

1 I began ...
2 I remember ...
3 I wasn't very good at ...
4 I was very talented at ...
5 I used to ...
6 I've never regretted ...
7 I decided to ...
8 I managed to ...
9 I've never really stopped ...
10 I was determined to ...
11 I have always succeeded in ...
12 I couldn't imagine ...
13 It's worth ...
14 I'm very proud of ...

5 Exchange information

Talk to a partner about your experiences, using any of the phrase openings from task 4.

6 Read and find out

The sentences below form a summary of part of a young woman's life. With a partner, put the sentences into a possible sequence and then combine them with these linking words:

as a result ...   as a consequence ...   although ...
even though ...   as ...   because ...

(1) Ruth was only just 16 when she suffered a stroke that left her paralysed.

( ) She has had to lower some of her ambitions.

( ) Her parents decided to push her as far as she could go.

( ) She forgot everything she had learnt during the previous two years.

( ) She has regained the sense of feeling in her leg and arm.

( ) She had wanted to do languages but she couldn't any more.

( ) She has sufficiently recovered to begin a law degree at university.

7 Read and write

Read the story in small groups. Stop after every paragraph and write a question related to what you have been reading, for example: How many doctors did she consult?

Learning a new quality: patience

Ruth was only just 16 when she suffered a stroke caused by a burst blood clot in her brain that left her paralysed. She had been having headaches for three months before the stroke and every time she went to the doctors they just told her to take paracetamol. She lost all movement on her right side, her speech, the sight in her right eye and her balance and memory went, too.

1:

After spending five days in intensive care, she underwent intensive physiotherapy and made, at first, quite a dramatic recovery. Her parents, along with her doctors, decided to push her as far as she could go so that her life would be affected as little as possible. She went back to boarding school in a wheelchair, unable to dress herself. That was awful to begin with, along with the problem of having forgotten all she had learnt during the previous two years.

2:

She used to be clever, ambitious, a keen musician and a talented tennis player. Now, she had to change her A-level subjects. She had wanted to do languages but she couldn't any more because of the short-term memory problems. However, she managed to do French which she had started a year earlier and had almost completed before the stroke. She also chose English literature and history.

3:

Not recognising friends at school was probably the worst thing for Ruth in the first six months. It was horrible. And when she made new friends, people made funny comments like, "You never liked her before". Ruth felt she had to start a new phase in her life. There are a few things she isn't able to do any more, like playing the piano and tennis. Sadly, she isn't allowed to play the oboe either because it puts too much pressure on the blood vessels and that is a problem if you have a weakness.

4:

8 Discuss and make your point

Compare your questions in class. If you like, try to answer them. Speculate and argue if necessary.

9 🔊 Listen and discuss

Listen to the end of Ruth's story. Which questions from 'Tune in' would she be happy to answer, do you think? Give reasons.

10 Put meaning into words

With a partner, think of and write down two more associated words to match each of the following key words (in colour), e.g.: save time (money/energy/water)

1 a look of disgust
2 feel embarrassed
3 slight idea
4 shout in excitement
5 intensive care
6 short-term memory
7 golden opportunity
8 rebellious children
9 average person
10 challenging job
11 previous years
12 practically perfect

Language in action

1 Exchange information

How much have you learnt since you left school?
First, write a list, for example:
I've learnt to drive a car.
I've taken part in a computer course.
I've attended several language courses.
I've done a training course in ...

Then read your list out in small groups. The others
should find out more by asking
How many ... have you ...? When did you ...?

2 Ask and answer

Choose a picture on p. 25 which reminds you most of
a place you have been to. Show the picture to your
partner and say where you went. Your partner then
tries to imagine the scene and tells you what you did
there. Here's an example:
– *I've been to an island.*
– *Well, you went swimming every day. You read a
 lot. You ...*

3 Write and exchange information

Write down a sentence about anything you did
when you were a teenager. Then dictate your
sentences to each other in groups of four. After that,
get up with your notes and ask at least three
students whether they did any of the things listed.
Try to find out more about your partners'
experiences. Finally, report to the class what you've
been told.

4 Read and find out

Complete these sentences and then exchange your
notes with a partner. Ask each other questions to
find out more. Try to use the right tenses.
1 I've always been interested in ...
2 I've never been keen on ...
3 I've always loved ...
4 I've always wanted to ...
5 I've never been talented at ...
6 I've always hoped to ...

5 Listen and react

Sit in groups of three. Each group takes one phrase from
below and completes it as many times as possible. The
others listen carefully and at the end try to repeat all the
situations mentioned, repeating the whole sentences.
1 I clearly remember ...
  e.g. *I clearly remember walking to school.*
    I clearly remember learning to drive.
2 I don't regret having ...
3 I've never really stopped ...

6 Make your point

Jane talks about repeated past habits and actions,
for example: *Everybody would say to me "School
days are the best days of your life." I would look at
them in horror.*
Face a partner. Work through the following situations
and tell your partner what you believe he/she did
in each of them. Use your imagination. Your partner
just listens and only reacts and corrects your
speculations at the end.
1 Whenever you got your pocket money you
  would ...
2 Whenever you had an exam the next day you
  would ...
3 Whenever you had bad marks you would ...
4 Whenever you had long holidays you would ...
5 Whenever your parents were away you would ...
6 Whenever you had no money but needed some
  you would ...

7 Discuss and write

What advice would you give young people of today?
Remember the people from Units 3 and 4.
In small groups, add more recommendations to the
list, completing each of the verbs in bold print.
1 In order to learn you **must** want to.
2 You **don't need to** stop work when you have a family.
3 You **need to** make progress very early to become
  chief executive.
4 You **have to** move between companies fast to
  gain international experience.

Shaping up for life

Unit 5 Unlocking your energy
Unit 6 Behind the glamour

Which of the questions below would you find interesting to ask each of the people in the pictures? With a partner, choose one question per person only. Don't use any question twice. Then discuss your ideas in class and suggest some possible answers the people in the pictures might give. Finally, in pairs choose two questions you would like to ask your teacher.

1 When and where do you feel most comfortable?
2 What effect does physical exercise or sport have on you?
3 What makes you feel good?
4 What does 'old age' make you think of?
5 Does your appearance play an important role in your life or job?
6 Do you like dressing up for special occasions?
7 To what extent is fashion important to you?
8 Are you easily influenced by fashion trends?

Unit 5 Unlocking your energy

1 🔊 Tune in

Sit comfortably and, if you like, close your eyes while listening to some relaxing music. Then, share your impressions in small groups. What impact has the music had on you? Did you see any pictures, did you hear any sounds or experience anything with your other senses? Did you see yourself in any of the pictures? What were you doing there?

2 Read and make your choice

The following advertisement shows an amazing new approach which is supposed to release the hidden talents and abilities we all have. Tick any of the suggested cassettes on offer that sound attractive to you. What kind of recorded material would you expect to hear on these topics? Talk to a partner.

At last, it's possible to release the genius within you!

These exclusive vocal coded 'Self-Learning' cassettes are unlike any you've heard before. They will inspire and revitalise you, they will help you achieve more and be more successful than you have ever thought possible. Thousands of people of all ages are achieving startling results. Just a glance at our offer shows you that our cassettes can help you in so many ways.

Order today by fax or phone, 0161 928 8181.

Please send me the following cassette(s) at £ 9.95 each.

- ☐ Weight Reduction
- ☐ Unlimited Mental Ability
- ☐ Better Concentration
- ☐ Power Memory
- ☐ Stop Smoking and Be Healthy
- ☐ Fitness Motivation
- ☐ Enthusiasm and Energy
- ☐ Positive Self Image
- ☐ Success at Financial Prosperity
- ☐ Increasing Self Awareness
- ☐ Attracting the Opposite Sex
- ☐ Stress Management

3 Read and use these expressions

There are numerous books and institutions suggesting methods to keep our physical and mental vitality alive. In small groups, answer the headlines of the two following advertisements. Then read the texts and discuss them in class. Would any of the two texts attract the attention of people with particular problems, do you think? Use these expressions.

There are exceptions, of course.   But don't forget ... .
But then again ... .   Let's not forget ... .

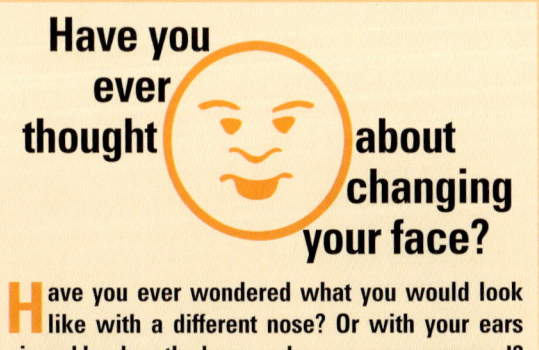

Have you ever thought about changing your face?

Have you ever wondered what you would look like with a different nose? Or with your ears pinned back or the bags under your eyes removed? What about the possible effects of a facelift, cheek implants or a chin correction? Or could you imagine yourself ten years younger with a few facelifts or wrinkle improvements?

For a free copy of our full colour information guide, please telephone 0181 577 99644 (today)!

Have you ever tried food for your vitality?

'The best diet for your life.' This book is a result of twenty years' research and is an effective guide to a happier, healthier future. Its eight-point diet plan provides new hope for those who are feeling depressed and who have been suffering from chronic illnesses. Choose the diet best suited to your life-style.

4 🔊 Listen and write

Six people aged between 84 and 102 have their own philosophy about a healthy life style. Your teacher will stop the tape after each person. With a partner, write down one more sentence the person might have said. Share your ideas and give reasons.

5 Discuss and make your point

How do you keep your body tuned and your mind in shape? As 84-year-old Jonathan said, "A little regular exercise can give you joy and satisfaction." What else can you gain from it? With a partner, write down more ideas and then discuss them in class.

6 Read and share your ideas

The two articles below appeared in an educational magazine. Which part(s) of the first text do you agree with most? Underline them. Have you had a similar experience? Share your thoughts in small groups.

Gaining energy to enjoy life

People who get regular physical exercise are usually happier, more relaxed and more alert. When you're fit and healthy, you'll find you look and feel better, too. Exercise can also help reduce stress levels or enable you to handle your stress better. With every training session you gain more and more energy and self-confidence. There's no doubt that physical exercise gives you a sense of achievement. As a result you feel good about yourself, knowing that you have improved your fitness and appearance. People who exercise regularly find they have more energy to enjoy life; it puts them in a better mood. Feelings of frustration or anger are replaced by feelings of calm or contentment.

7 Exchange information, put meaning into words and write

Work with a partner. Student A look at page 75, student B at page 77. First, read your words to each other and try to form matching pairs. Then, write a short text for an educational magazine on the value of team sports. Use as many of your word combinations as possible and add a headline, too.

8 Read and make your choice

Do you agree with the statements below? Discuss in small groups and give examples. Then decide where you would best place each of them in the text that follows. They can go in any order. At the end, compare your results.

1 Working as a team to solve problems and face difficulties together builds up courage and confidence.
2 Playing in a team can improve your social life.
3 Being dependent on the other members of the team, with others depending on you, gives a sense of security and belonging.
4 Being a good team member is a useful skill for getting along with your family.

Building up courage and confidence

Training and playing as a team is a skill in itself. Learning how to co-operate with others, to find your own special place in the group and to make decisions with members of the group are skills you need in various areas of your life. It is also important when you finish school and get a job. Members of a team help each other, supporting and encouraging the weaker members and backing up the stronger ones. A team will quickly develop its own identity, with members taking pride in the team's achievements and feeling great loyalty towards one another. It is a rewarding experience to know that you are part of a successful team. Apart from that, it is a challenge to be struggling to win! Meeting new people with similar interests can lead to new friendships. Teams often like to socialise together away from the game, especially when they are celebrating a win.

Unit 6　Behind the glamour

1 Tune in

Imagine you have been invited to a friend's party. You have just walked into a room packed with strangers who are standing in groups deep in conversation. A number of guests are elegantly dressed, others quite casually. Some of them seem to be enjoying themselves. Would you approach any of these people? Who would you choose to talk to? How would you introduce yourself? Tell a partner what you would do.

2 Discuss and write

What do these four people look like, do you think? Imagine their ages and faces. Decide on their personalities, interests, jobs and characters, too. Who would you like to share an evening with? Choose one only and discuss in small groups. Take some notes and describe your person to the class. These phrases can help you.

The person is ... / looks ... / looks like ... / looks as if ... / appears to be ...

3 Use these expressions and put meaning into words

Think of a person you feel at ease with. Tell your partner what it is you appreciate about his or her personality and character. Then describe the kind of person you feel uncomfortable with. Let your partner do the same. Write down the adjectives he/she uses and compare them in class.

I quite / particularly like the way he/she ...　　　I don't particularly like ...
I very much appreciate his / her / the way he/she ...　　I can't stand / bear ...

4 Read and share your ideas

The four women described below are all looking for a partner. Who do you think is the nicest or the most interesting of them all? Who might look the most beautiful or attractive? Which of them is the most sporty or active person, would you say? Discuss.

E N C O U N T E R S

Female 24, nurse, charming person, loves meeting people, countryside, theatre, pubs, eating out and music, is looking for that special person to care for and share happy moments with, sharp mind is more important than age. 0839 108

Female early 50s, slim and attractive widow, self-supporting, good conversationalist, attractive mind, enjoys music, reading and outings, would like interesting and understanding partner to visit places and share various activities with. 0839 103

Female 19, blonde, attractive, classy, good at cooking, loves humour, charm, motor bikes, trips abroad and tennis, is looking for active and adventurous partner to share interests and fun, possible marriage. 0839 101

Female 39, divorced, warm-hearted, stylish, 2 children and a dog, enjoys classical music, art and having guests, would like to meet sociable, ambitious and caring man to share friendship and romance. 0839 102

5 ◀)) Listen and make your choice

'Date-line' is an agency which helps people find a partner by means of recorded voices. Listen and after each introduction discuss in small groups which of the four women suits the candidate best. Finally compare your results giving reasons.

6 Discuss

What do these statements have in common? Which would you consider to be true?

1 Some people believe you are what you eat. Others say you are what you wear.
2 If you change the outside, it also changes the inside.

7 Read and make your point

Brand names like *Cardin*, *Benetton*, *Adidas*, *Lacoste* and *Boss* are internationally well-known. They stand for good quality and for a good price, too. Work with a partner and tick all the answers that best suit the 'Boss Man'. Compare and discuss your results.

1 What does a 'Boss' suit look like?

a ☐ like an elegant evening suit
b ☐ like leisure wear
c ☐ like a working suit for managers
d ☐ fashionable

2 Who is the 'Boss' customer?

a ☐ a good-looking man
b ☐ a business man
c ☐ a playboy
d ☐ a show-off

3 What's the 'Boss' man like?

a ☐ masculine
b ☐ successful
c ☐ common
d ☐ authoritative
e ☐ sophisticated
f ☐ non-smoker
g ☐ has a good sense of humour
h ☐ likes sports
i ☐ intelligent
k ☐ proud

8 Read and discuss

Compare your answers to the above questionnaire with this text. Do you agree?

Style is never out of fashion

Do you sometimes look a mess? Do your outfits lead people to think you are colour-blind? Or are you a fashion slave even though fashions don't suit you?

For a number of years now, 'Boss' has been one of the biggest brand names in menswear in Germany and among the top labels in Europe. The brand name, or so the 'Boss' people believe, stands for 'masculinity, authority and success'. The 'Boss' customer is the man who values the look of a designer label. In full-page ads the 'Boss' male always stands (he seldom sits) – proud, elegant, often alone. The 'Boss' man has a strong personality, and he doesn't smoke. His image is of a clean-living person, who plays a little golf or tennis. Rugby would be totally wrong for this brand of male image.

You may think that fashion is only for the rich. But it is no secret that the Italian sense of style makes roadsweepers in Rome look as though they have stepped out of an Armani shop window. Is it true that the way we dress reflects personal self-worth and esteem? Many individuals are happy to look a total mess. I wonder why!

9 Discuss and use these expressions

Which of the sayings on the right would you particularly connect with the 'Boss' man? Discuss in small groups. Then share your opinion in more general terms.

In general ...
On the whole ...
By and large ...
As a rule ...
Generally speaking ...
One can say that ...

1 A good horse is never of a bad colour.
2 A monkey remains a monkey though dressed in silk.
3 A smart coat is a good letter of introduction.
4 As a man dresses so is he esteemed.
5 Every picture tells a story.
6 Fine feathers make a fine bird.
7 In one country your name, in other countries your appearance.

Language in action

1 Put meaning into words

Read through the list of verbs and think of a situation you were in that matches one of them. Then share your experience with a partner.

1 I intended to …
2 I dared to …
3 I failed to …
4 I was forced to …
5 I decided to …
6 I hesitated to …
7 I forgot to …
8 I hoped to …
9 I refused to …
10 I arranged to …

2 Make your choice

Choose a person you don't particularly like from any picture in this book. In small groups, introduce this person as your neighbour, expressing your anger about his/her general misconduct, like this:
This is my neighbour. He/She is always having parties and is continually making lots of noise. He/She is constantly complaining about his/her health.

3 Write and react

Try to remember a specific happy or exciting moment you experienced sometime in the past. Write down when it was and what you were doing at that very moment. Then, exchange your notes with a partner, who will continue your story in your name. Finally, exchange notes again, read and talk about the results. Here's an example: *It was in September 1994. I was celebrating my 50th birthday with all my friends.*

4 Read and exchange information

Divide the class into two groups. Group A turn to page 75, group B look at page 77. Read your article and in pairs each write down four comprehension questions on a slip of paper. Then sit with a partner from the other group. Exchange your questions and try to answer them using your imagination. Don't correct your partner's answers nor give any hints. At the end, read each other's story.

5 Discuss and write

In small groups choose two of the following headlines. What other information might the article include? Add one or more sentences, using these phrase openings.

While …   As long as …   As soon as …
Whenever …   By the time …   It was not until …

> **As women are trying to find better job satisfaction, men take over new roles.**
>
> **19-year-old Sue has been travelling around Europe in a wheelchair for three months.**
>
> **Holidaymakers had been waiting for hours before the planes could finally take off.**
>
> **Greenpeace people were demonstrating against the transport of nuclear waste.**
>
> **Prices will continually be rising during the coming year.**

6 Share your ideas

Imagine you are sitting at the airport amongst the passengers in the picture, waiting to board the plane which has been delayed for three hours.
With a partner or on your own, write a short poem expressing your situation. What are you doing or thinking about, how are you or some of the people feeling? Here's an example.

I've been patiently sitting here
for two hours or maybe three.
And I'm watching all the people
who will be boarding the plane with me.
Some of them are reading,
or seem to be doing so.
Their minds are probably wandering –
to the place they're going to go.

Topic **4**

In search of personal freedom

Unit 7 Taking a break
Unit 8 A gap in a life

Which of these places do you feel most attracted by? Choose one only.

If you spent a day or more there, what exactly would you do?
In what way would this environment offer you a change from your everyday routine?

Unit 7   Taking a break

1 Tune in
Reflect on these questions first. Then sit in small groups and answer them.
If you were a season of the year, which season would you be? Why?
If you were a month of the year, which month would you be? Why?
If you were a country or part of the countryside, which would you be? Why?

2 Read and use these expressions
In the following extracts three different types of people talk about their preferences when travelling. Are they male or female, do you think? Which of these people would you most likely share a holiday with?

Decide on one person only and discuss in small groups. Give reasons and express your reservations. Use these expressions:

Provided that ...   As long as ...   Unless ...
On condition that ...   If ...

1 *"I particularly enjoy countryside with rolling hills, but that is not too gentle. Best of all is the moment when mountains come into view and you know you're going to go up and over into wonderful valleys. I love the way the weather is constantly changing there. You'll get bright, clear light in the morning, then the clouds will move smoothly along and in a matter of minutes the sky will look as though somebody has pulled a cover over you. By the evening it will have changed again and there will be little puffy pink clouds dancing on the sunset."*

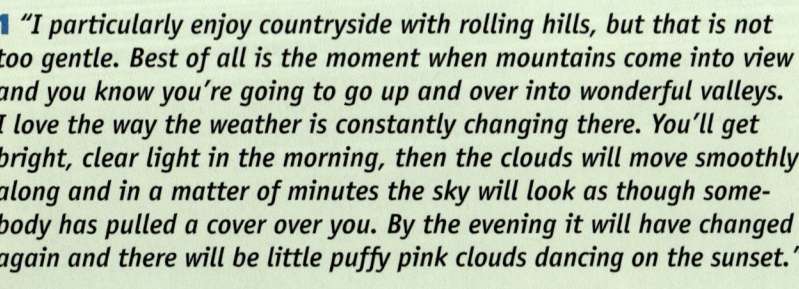

2 *"I use holidays to clear my head and get a perspective on things. As long as I feel I'm benefiting from it on some level, I can go anywhere. I don't consider my own country a holiday destination as I want to become familiar with Europe or other continents. I'm quite keen on visiting places of interest and I like to have a new experience every year. Provided the programme is interesting, I even accept package tours, which can be great and require little effort when planning."*

3 *"I tend not to plan my route because I think that things happen when you allow them to. I've never been on a package holiday and I can't imagine enjoying one. And I wouldn't enjoy a holiday if it was luxurious – I'd just put something on my back and go – take whatever comes. I once travelled in the back of a pick-up truck and slept under the stars. I don't think I washed thoroughly for three weeks. I felt a changed person after that holiday"*

3 Exchange information
You all work on a market survey for 'Enterprise', a well-known travel agent. Divide the class into two groups. Group A works on the questions 1-3, group B on the questions 4-6. Get up and interview each other forming A/B-pairs several times. Take notes and compare your results in class later.

1 How do you usually feel before going on holiday?
2 Do you ever travel alone?
3 Is one suitcase enough for a two-week holiday?
4 What kind of accommodation do you prefer?
5 How do you relax best during your holidays?
6 What effect does a good holiday have on you?

4 🔊 Listen and react
Ann Baker is being questioned by an 'Enterprise' staff member. Listen and take some notes. If you were forced to spend some days together with Ann, what problems – if any – would you have to face, do you think? Would you get on well with her? Why?/Why not?
Talk to a partner. "If I had to spend some days together with Ann, I would most probably ..."

5 Discuss

What does a good holiday mean for you? Which was the worst holiday you have ever had? Which picture do you have in mind when you think of it? Describe it to your partner.

6 Put meaning into words

Tick all those words which remind you of your holidays. Then share your experience with a partner.

- ☐ luxurious
- ☐ unpleasant
- ☐ vast expense
- ☐ nervous wreck
- ☐ strange food

- ☐ magical
- ☐ calculated
- ☐ amuse myself
- ☐ invigorate
- ☐ misunderstandings

- ☐ ridiculous
- ☐ tensions
- ☐ tip everyone
- ☐ horrid
- ☐ family togetherness

- ☐ holiday ritual
- ☐ jealousies
- ☐ unwind
- ☐ outbursts of bad temper
- ☐ pretend huge enjoyment

7 Read and find out

The words above are taken from the following text. What kind of experience did the author have, do you think? Did he enjoy it?

....
....

This year we have transported ourselves to a luxurious hideaway in the Swiss Alps, complete with swimming pool, waterfall, lake and choice of mountains. You'll forgive me, I hope, but I am already counting the days until I can utter the most magical words in the English language: "It's time to go home."
I cannot be alone in finding every aspect of the holiday ritual to be utterly ridiculous and unpleasant. Unless you are a millionaire, it is impossible to be as comfortable on holiday as at home. As for family togetherness: forget it. It is hard to imagine a situation more calculated to introduce tensions, jealousies, misunderstandings and outbursts of bad temper.
At home, I can eat what I want and when I want. On holiday, I must eat strange food at vast expense at times determined by someone else. I am then expected to amuse myself in a swimming costume, speak foreign languages, tip everyone in sight

and simultaneously pretend huge enjoyment. We go on holiday to unwind, and return as nervous wrecks. We claim that the fresh air and sun will invigorate us, but return with our bodies tanned to the first stage of melanoma. We then count ourselves lucky if we see our baggage again, the house has not been burgled and the teenager next door has remembered to feed the cat.
We have somehow become persuaded that this horrid and costly experience is central to our happiness, yet there is not a piece of evidence to support this proposition. What is the source of the taboo? Why are we so hesitant to admit the truth? Why, when we return from holiday, do we lie to our colleagues, telling them what a wonderful time we had? As long as we believe in nothing else, we have to persuade ourselves that a week or two away is the answer to everything.

8 Discuss and make your point

To what extent can you agree with the author's point of view? Discuss in class.

9 Discuss and write

Read through the text again and with a partner copy several short phrases which could generally serve as sensational headlines in newspapers. Then, sit in groups of four and choose one that would be most suitable for this text. If you like, use your list to make a kind of poem. Here's an example:

Luxurious hideaway in the Swiss Alps
Choice of mountains
Strange food at vast expense
Fresh air and sun.

Unit 8   A gap in a life

1 Tune in

Could you imagine taking a two- or three-month holiday? Or would you even allow yourself to take a whole year off? What obligations, commitments or personal reasons would hinder you from leaving your present situation? Talk to a partner.

- ☐ family
- ☐ education
- ☐ money
- ☐ security
- ☐ health
- ☐ courage
- ☐ job
- ☐ age
- ☐ ...

2 🔊)) Listen and discuss

Listen to the poem first with your books closed. How old do you think the person is? What's her general attitude towards a 'year off'? What seems important for her? Which of the facts in 'Tune in' might stop her from taking a year off? Discuss in small groups first and then in class.

3 Read and make your choice

Do you partly share the writer's opinion? Which of the verses reflect your own dreams and needs? Choose and explain in small groups.

A Year Out

I wish I had a year to spend
with nothing much to do,
I could pursue any interest
and share more time with you.

I've never taken a year off,
I wish I could have done;
and in a way – I envy
the people who are young.

I'd study other cultures
if I had a year to spend;
I'd take a room in Paris
and share it with a friend.

I'd learn another language
to find if people care
about the world around them
and how they feel and share.

I would travel in great comfort,
enjoy the wine and the food;
I'd always be in good company
and show the best of my mood.

Though I'd probably feel guilty
to lose a year of mine;
I'd rather be where I should be
and not waste such precious time.

I wouldn't want to be restless,
and on the move each day;
I'd rather live every minute
instead of rushing away.

4 Read and find out

Oliver Banks used to work as a head of children's programmes on television. Read and compare the poem with this text. What do the two people have in common? Do they share any interests or opinions? Work in small groups and take some notes. Compare in class later.

I regret not having had a year off. I think it would have given me more perspective on life. I'm too old now to muck about in Land Rovers, but I think I might have headed for the Antarctic. As an alternative, I would have felt quite tempted to spend some time in the jungle in Ecuador. I would definitely have enjoyed going to out-of-the-way places that are off the normal beaten track. I'd never have wanted to get a round-the-world ticket – as young students do – because they all end up in exactly the same places, like Bangkok or Sydney. I would have stayed away from the tourists, eaten in local restaurants, met the locals and sampled their way of life.

I wish I could have gone abroad and experienced another culture, like in India, for example. I would have appreciated the quiet pace of life and the sense of being in a totally different world. If money had been no object, I might well have gone in a Land Rover, moving around Europe and finding out how people lived.

In my younger years I once went to help set up a play scheme for fifty disturbed children with Community Service Volunteers. Looking back now, provided I had been able to take a year out, I would have liked to have done something like VSO, to have gone and worked in a Third World country.

But I'm 67 now and I really like my way of life. I have a lot of things I want to do and it's wonderful to be able to pursue anything you are interested in, particularly as I don't need to earn a living any more. I still feel alert enough to take advantage of all the possibilities offered. The more I think about a fantasy year, the more I feel that there are other things I could perhaps spend my time doing.

⇨ Cultural information, p. 81

5 Discuss and use these expressions

What might have stopped Oliver from taking a year off, do you think? Consider the points in 'Tune in' and give reasons, making assumptions.
He might (not) have wanted to ...
He could have had to ...
He must have ...
He needn't necessarily have had to ...

6 Put meaning into words

Divide the class into two groups. Group A writes possible definitions of the coloured words in sentences 1-5; group B does the same with the words in sentences 6-10. Work in small groups and use a monolingual dictionary if necessary.
Then form A/B pairs. Read your definitions in mixed order to your partner, who tries to find the corresponding expressions.

1 would have given me more perspective on life
2 I'm too old now to muck about
3 I might have headed for the Antarctic
4 I would have felt quite tempted to spend some time in the jungle
5 that are off the normal beaten track
6 meet the locals and sample their way of life
7 I would have appreciated the quiet pace of life
8 if money had been no object
9 it's wonderful to be able to pursue anything you are interested in
10 I still feel alert enough to take advantage of all the possibilities offered

Language in action

1 Share your ideas

Your teacher collects one particular or interesting item from every student and hands them out again at random. Look at it carefully and one by one say how you would have felt and what you would have done with it, like this:

If I had received this/these ... as a present, I would have felt ... . / I would probably (not) have ...

2 Listen and react

Sit in small groups. Imagine you had one of the problems listed below. Tell the others about it and listen to their comments. Look at the example and react in the same way. Use your imagination.

– *If I had been in your situation I'd certainly (not) have (done) ...*
– *Yes, but if I had (not) (done) ... I'd probably ...*

1 My friend arrived late at the airport, so we both missed the plane.
2 My suitcase arrived three days after arrival. I had already bought some new clothes.
3 I had booked a quiet hotel but it turned out to be on a busy road.
4 I had very little money when I was young and couldn't afford to travel abroad.
5 My family desperately wanted a dog, but now it's me who has to take care of it.
6 I invited some important guests but unfortunately the new dish I had prepared wasn't very tasty.

3 Make your choice and write

With a partner, choose a picture out of the picture page of Topic 4 on page 25. Imagine you were on holiday there right now. Write a postcard to the two students on your right, including the phrases and words below in any order you like. Begin and end in the usual way. Exchange your cards and read some of them to the class.

if the place were ...   it would be ...   unless ...
provided that ...   as long as ...

4 Exchange information

Complete the following phrase openings twice each. Then form small groups and compare your wishes, giving reasons. How many wishes do you have in common? For example: *I wish I lived in a southern country. If only my parents had been bilingual.*
I wish / If only I were (did) ...
I wish / If only I had (done) ...

5 Read and find out

Write down five things you did last month which don't belong to your everyday routine. Then exchange your list with a partner and ask each other questions. Here's an example:

– *I took a train to Frankfurt.*
– *What would have happened if you hadn't taken a train to Frankfurt?*
– *If I hadn't taken that train, I might not have met my friend.* or: *I would have arrived too late for the meeting.*

6 Read and write

Look at the picture which appeared in yesterday's newspaper. In groups of three, write the end of the article, including these structures.
should / must / could / might (not) have (done)
ought (not) to have (done)

Another traffic disaster

Due to heavy traffic there was yet another accident on the M2 on Monday evening. A spokesman said that traffic had been moving at normal speed when a lorry came to a sudden stop. More than ten cars were finally involved in the accident and two people died before the ambulance could make its way through the lanes to rescue the victims. Police claim that ...

Topic 5

Keeping up with the media

Unit 9 The electronic screen
Unit 10 Plugged into scary facts

If each of the individual pictures on the film strip represented the main feature of a film, which film would you most likely choose to see? Give reasons.
What influence do pictures and the media have on society?
What other words do you relate to the pictures 2, 3 and 4 apart from 'information'?

2

3 *Who stole my baby?*

If you love her, give her back

4

31

Unit 9   The electronic screen

1 Tune in
First, answer these questions in pairs. Then, write down three more questions that cover the same topics (leisure time, TV, radio, newspapers). Exchange your notes with another pair and answer again.

1 What does 'having a good time' mean to you?
2 What embarrasses you most when watching TV?
3 How do you keep up with what is happening in the world around you?

2 Discuss and use these expressions
The following statements are the result of a survey on Media Futures. Express your belief or disbelief by adding the numbers 1 or 2 to each. Then discuss in small groups.

1 I rather doubt it. / That's very unlikely.
2 There's no doubt about it. / I'm quite sure about it.

☐ There is a growing public discontent with television.
☐ People are watching less, and getting less pleasure from what they see.
☐ Older people tend to watch more TV than the average viewers.
☐ Activities like watching pre-recorded videos or playing computer games have become the major pastime for children.
☐ Radio listening has increased significantly over the past few years.
☐ The more intelligent and better-off people are far more likely to be interested in radio or newspapers.
☐ The fall in readership of the press is unexpectedly heavy particularly among the young.
☐ Over the next few years one could expect the present dominance of the electronic screen to decrease.

3 🔊 Read, put meaning into words and listen
Work with a partner and fill in the blanks of this newspaper article with the figures and expressions listed. Discuss your results in class first. Then listen to part of a radio programme and check your answers.

one third / a great deal / an average amount / 75 per cent / a great number /
a large number / every second / one in every four / 5 per cent / an astonishing number.

A TV in the bedroom and cash to spend

The findings of a recent survey reveal that .... of today's children have money in their pockets and televisions in their bedrooms. Children's spending power is rising ...., as particularly for older children, pocket money is not the only source of income. .... of those over 11 has a job of some kind. The survey also mentions that .... of children worry about the environment and .... prefer dangerous sports. Watching television is the favourite pastime, with a lot of children watching .... of three hours a day. Astonishingly, results show that .... of the children like going to school. .... seem to agree that homework is important and about .... child spends at least an hour doing it. But nearly .... admit that they rarely bother to do it.

4 🔊 Listen and discuss
Listen to the rest of the radio programme. Do you share the mother's opinion? What are the advantages and disadvantages of individual TV sets and videos? What might a child's bedroom in the year 2010 look like?

5 Share your ideas

Find an answer to these questions and then compare in class.

Could you give up your TV set for life?

How much compensation would you demand if you weren't allowed to watch television any more?

6 Read, use these expressions and write

Form four groups or pairs. Each group or pair reads one of the four paragraphs in the article on the right. Imagine you were the author of your paragraph. Discuss and write one or two additional sentences, taking your opinion into consideration. Use phrases like:

Bearing in mind (that) ...

When you consider (that) ...

Allowing for the fact that ...

Taking into account (that) ...

Finally, read your complete text to the class.

Could you do without it?

In an astonishing survey, 15 per cent of people, nearly one in seven, admitted that even if they were offered a million pounds they wouldn't part with their televisions. But one third believed they'd give it up for just 10,000 pounds.

A ☐ Yet, other reports show that a number of parents believe that their children learn a great deal from watching TV. They think that their children know more about the country and the world than previous generations ever did. Some parents even argue that TV provides better discussions than most family dinner tables. At the same time they admit that children are bombarded by information of all kinds; ideas, views and experiences which go far beyond anything people are ever likely to encounter in real life. ...

B ☐ Is TV getting worse? People always think so. In last year's survey, for example, 29 per cent thought television had got worse, though 11 per cent were still convinced it had improved. A considerable number of people did not believe TV provided value for money.

Another survey showed that a third of people shout back at the TV set. One in five said they talked to the TV, continuing a debate or talking to characters. But only a small number of people admitted they had once picked up the phone to complain. ...

C ☐ The average amount of leisure time for adults is 35 hours a week and for a great number of people watching television is virtually their only leisure pursuit. The overall viewing figures show that we watch an average of 25 hours a week, not including the added hours people now spend watching rented videos. Some people claim that they hardly watch any TV, presumably because they are the sort to plan their viewing selectively. But others confess that they are indiscriminate channel-hoppers or even leave the set on all day. ...

D ☐ A very recent report criticised the sloppy speech of children's TV presenters. But poor speech was only one symptom, they said. It was argued that an astonishing number of performers actually made fun of learning. The report continued by saying that, although TV had once been praised as the great new educational tool, there was little sign of expanding horizons. They wondered where the role models on children's television were. ...

7 Discuss and make your choice

If this were a complete article, in what order would you want the paragraphs to appear? Decide in small groups and add the numbers. What other topics could relate to the same headline? Discuss.

Unit 10 Plugged into scary facts

1 Tune in

What kind of stories are behind each of the film titles below? A war, a crime story, a western, a love story or even a comedy? Which of these films would a teenager of about 14 choose to see? Which would an elderly person prefer? Discuss in small groups and give reasons.

The Man with one Red Shoe	The Victim	Song of the South
Love is a wonderful colour	Mask	The Killing Fields
The Thief of Baghdad	Black Rain	Until the Break of Day

2 Discuss and use these expressions

We have already become accustomed to the type of headlines in our daily newspapers which reveal the danger and negative impact new technology can have on society, particularly on the young generation. What kind of dangers do the headlines below refer to, do you think? Share your ideas, expressing your conviction. Use these expressions.

I honestly feel that ... I strongly believe that ...
I am convinced that ... I'm absolutely certain that ...

Parents increasingly fear for the safety of their children

Hard-core pornography on-line

Anger over Internet shooting game

Boy driven to suicide by boredom

CHILDREN'S NIGHTMARES

VIOLENT VIDEOS CAUSE CRIME

Weekly Cruelties of the Real-Life News

3 Read and exchange information

While parents fear for the safety of their children, their offspring are frightened, too. But not only about the weekly disasters of the real-life news.
Discuss these questions in class and express your opinion.
1 What are children most scared of?
2 How do they react towards the daily TV news?
3 To what extent do children like being scared?
4 When do children feel most secure?

Three schoolchildren, Olivia, aged seven, Philip, aged nine, and Katie, aged twelve, expressed their worries and fears they encounter day by day. Form three groups. Group A turn to page 75, group B to page 77 and group C to page 79. Read your text in pairs and answer the questions, considering the child in your text. Take individual notes.
Once everybody is ready, form A/B/C groups and answer the questions with the help of your notes only. What do the three children have in common?

4 Put meaning into words

Look back at the three texts and copy the words the children used to express various degrees of fear. Put them in order according to their degrees and complete the list adding an adjective or noun wherever possible.

I feel	something is	noun
scared	scary	scare
...	...	...

5 Discuss

What kind of news are children generally frightened of when watching television? Is it the news itself or the picture which strikes them most, do you think?

WHY KIDNAPPER SNATCHED BABY NICOLA

AGONY OF MUM WHO LEFT TOT WITH EVIL CHILDMINDER

PUSHCHAIR FOUND AT VICTORIA BUS STATION

BABY SNATCHER TELLS HER PARENTS: I DID IT FOR YOU

SHE SEEMED SO NICE

She just wanted to make her mum and dad happy

THERE WAS NO THREAT

Parents torn by despair

END OF NIGHTMARE: JOURNEY TO REUNION WITH NICOLA

7 🔊 Discuss, write and listen

Shortly after the kidnapping, the news was also reported on TV. In what order did the actions of the first day take place, do you think? Work in groups and write a short paragraph about the events of the first day using the verbs listed below. Then listen to part of the TV news and check your notes.

were missing – were interviewed – was called – had been looked after – was kidnapped – should be reported – have been discovered

If you were a police officer, what questions would you ask Mrs Davies on the day of the kidnapping?

8 🔊 Listen and make your point

Now, listen to parts 1, 2 and 3 of the TV news that followed. After each part, in pairs write questions you would ask the following people and compare your results later.

Part 1: the passenger who recognised the kidnapper on the ferry boat to Dublin

Part 2: the police

Part 3: a) the kidnapper's parents after they had been told the truth

b) the kidnapper after having been arrested

6 Read and make your choice

A dramatic story took place in summer 1997. It all started with a small advertisement which appeared in The Times.

> **Mature person required** to do light housework and look after 6 month baby in East Ham area, references needed, £ 50 per week. Philippa

The story was reported over three days in various newspapers. Look at the headlines and, in groups of three, try to reconstruct what happened between Thursday 14th and Saturday 16th August.

WITNESSES TELL OF TALKING TO WOMAN ON NIGHT FERRY

Father tells of kidnapper's guilt at giving twins for adoption

Baby Nicola found alive in Ireland

We will do everything we can to help her

BABY NICOLA WELL LOOKED AFTER

9 🔊 Listen and share your ideas

While you are listening to the report a second time, imagine the pictures or film which might have accompanied the individual TV news items. After each part, discuss in small groups and describe your visions to the class.

35

Language in action

1 Exchange information

Do you like giving presents? Why? / Why not?
Now, think of a) the most expensive, b) the smallest, c) the most exciting present you have ever been given and describe it to a partner.
The smallest present I've ever been given was a ... .
It was given to me by ...

2 Put meaning into words

Work in small groups and match the following sentences with their definitions.

- [ ] a) I was kept in the dark.
- [ ] b) I was taken aback.
- [ ] c) I was carried away.
- [ ] d) I was worked up.
- [ ] e) I was worn out.
- [ ] f) I was put down.
- [ ] g) I was put right.
- [ ] h) I was looked up to.

1 excited	5 not informed
2 corrected	6 criticised
3 admired	7 surprised and confused
4 very tired	8 very upset esp. when worried

Then think of a moment you once experienced which corresponds to one of these situations. Mention it to your group. The others will then try to find out more by asking questions like this:
When exactly ...? Why ...? Was it the first time you ...? How often ...? Was it a good or a bad experience? Are you easily ...?

3 Exchange information and discuss

Yesterday, you received a letter from 'International TV-Corporation', ITC. Sit with a partner. Student A, look at page 76, student B turn to page 78. Report in detail what information your letter contains, using reported speech. Compare your contents without looking at each other's books. Then discuss.

4 Share your ideas

Have you read today's newspaper yet? Imagine there was a headline about you on the front page. Think of one that reveals something particular about you, your daily life, your future plans or about any experience you have had. Write the headline down and then read it out in small groups. Speculate on what the 'article' said about each of your partners. Use your imagination. Here's an example:

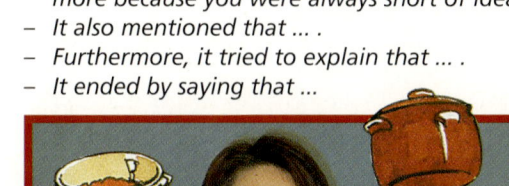

- – The article said that you didn't like cooking any more because you were always short of ideas.
- – It also mentioned that ... .
- – Furthermore, it tried to explain that ... .
- – It ended by saying that ...

5 Write and discuss

In your newspaper you also found an article on

No need to lift a finger in the automated world of the future.

With a partner, write down three things you believe will be done automatically in the future, either with the press of a button or by computer. Then share your ideas in groups of four. Discuss them later in class. Think about the facilities in the house, the car, shopping, banking, school, entertainment, etc., like this:
Lights will be switched on whenever I enter a room.

Topic 6

Living in a fast society

Unit 11   The techno-paradise
Unit 12   The streets of hope

Looking at these pictures, what contrasts can you find?
Write them down.
What problems come to mind when you think of a 'fast society'?

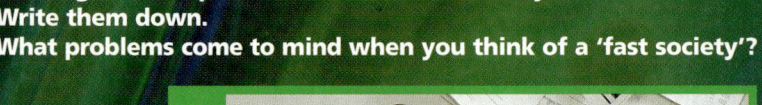

Unit 11 The techno-paradise

1 Tune in

What makes your daily work routine pleasant at times? Write down six factors which you consider to be relevant. Once you have decided, grade your list according to importance adding the numbers 1-6 (most - least relevant). Then compare in small groups.

2 Read and make your choice

Are you fed up with the rat race?
Bored with your working environment?
SPAIN OPENS VILLAGE ...

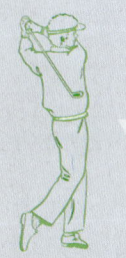

Spain may hold the answer to your problem. An abandoned hamlet is about to be reborn as the country's first computerised and international village, allowing inhabitants to link up with offices anywhere in the world from a restored and rural idyll. The village will be opening early next year.

For further details: Tel 0171 988 1011, Fax 0171 988 1111, e-mail: rural.digi@hispanoprovid.es, website: http://www.ruraldigi.es

Which of the following paragraphs would you add to the advertisement above in order to attract the attention of future buyers? Work in pairs and choose one paragraph only. Give reasons.

1 The group of 65 houses will be known as a 'telematic village' and will offer a new breed of villagers the chance to wheel and deal on global markets from the rough and hilly countryside. The Internet global network will allow you to work anywhere.

2 The natural beauty of the village may be the key attraction for you. Apart from magnificent views, each flat will offer permanent access to the Internet via a computer 'server', as well as cable and satellite TV and 'interactive television' services.

3 The future inhabitants will be able to shop on the Internet while holding video conferences with offices around the world; two cafes will be linked to computers and are expected to host cultural events.

3 Discuss and use these expressions

Many people are sceptical about the idea of the 'telematic village'. Others favour it. What do you think about it? Discuss in small groups and express your reservations by completing one of these phrase openings:.

I wonder whether ...   What I'd be worried about is ...
I don't see how ...   The problem really is ...

Now, read the following statements. Who are the people that expressed their opinion? Discuss and add the appropriate letter to each box: L = local, A = architect, T = telecommunication expert. Finally, choose the statements you disagree with and share your ideas in class.

☐ New technology is to allow people to move more freely, not tie them down to one place.
☐ The idea of the isolated Internet addict, glued to a laptop all day seems to be in contrast to the Spanish way of life.
☐ For this to be a success, the organisers will need to create a sense of identity and community which is difficult to achieve with business-oriented people.
☐ It will help reverse the flow of young people who went away from the area.
☐ The peaceful valley will not be turned upside down. Locals will obviously profit from increased trade.
☐ Once people move in, they will soon be missing busy city life.

4 Discuss

You are going to attend an international conference that deals with the topic 'Facing the Problems of a Fast Society'. What lectures do you expect to be on the programme? Write a list. What would you be most interested in? Discuss in groups.

5 Read, write and exchange information

In the conference brochure, you find a brief comment on a lecture called 'High Anxiety'. Form three groups. Each group reads one text only, text A, B, or C. With a partner from your group, write down two questions which your text makes you think of and which are interesting to talk about. Then discuss them in class.

High **Anxiety**

A Since the lift was invented in 1852, people have dreamt of a mile-high tower and wondered how to make it stand up. But technology isn't a problem any more. The real challenge facing us today is social, not technical. Can a modest half-mile tower which would contain as many people as Penzance be lived in? Will people be living in 'villages in the sky' with work places, playgrounds, day nurseries, shops, study areas, gardens, resting and partying places? To some people, of course, it sounds absolutely marvellous because it would mean no more commuting.

B On the other hand, the fact that there is air space available doesn't mean that it is right to build high. The impact of skyscrapers, made of steel, concrete and glass will change the life of a city for generations. Imagine a 200-storey high 'glass container' that is double the size of some of today's skyscrapers. It is a nightmare scenario. It is a battery farm for people, a city within the city. Every floor, every workplace, every flat, even every body looks the same. There are no open spaces for people to enjoy the fresh air. The environment is artificially controlled, with artificial air, artificial light, and artificial behaviour patterns.

C Impressed by the vastness of their creations, architects and designers of high buildings often overlook the humble people who have to live and work in skyscrapers. These creative humans plan amazing groupings of fascinating buildings which should guarantee the relationship between the inhabitants; it should guarantee air, light, and happiness, too. We call it the quality of life. Our culture needs masterplans that will focus more on the occupants and their way of life. Furthermore, developers of successful super-high buildings will have to consider time as well. If they cannot change, today's megatowers will risk being tomorrow's ghost towns.

6 Read and put meaning into words

With a partner, read the whole text and copy all the words and phrases you would personally need to describe a fictional future city. Compare your notes in class.

7 🔊)) Listen, discuss and write

You are going to hear an extract of Charles Dickens' (1812-1870) novel 'Hard Times', where he deals with the social and industrial problems of a new age and describes the industrialised city of Coketown. First listen without taking any notes. What's the relationship between the description above and the one on the CD?

Then, listen to some parts of the text again. Work with a partner. After each part, write a sentence describing similar aspects of a fictional future city with the help of your wordlist from task 6. Use your imagination as well. Finally, read your descriptions to the class.

It will be a city of ... / It will have ... / It will contain ... / It will be inhabited by ...

⟲ Cultural information, p. 81

Unit 12   The streets of hope

1 Tune in

Look at the picture of the Brazilian boy who collects used paper, plastic, rags and bottles from garbage dumps and sells them to retailers for recycling. Express your reaction by ticking the statements which describe your feelings best. Then share your thoughts in small groups and in class.

- ☐ I pity the child.
- ☐ I feel helpless.
- ☐ It reminds me of something I read about.
- ☐ It creates other pictures in my mind.
- ☐ I would like to talk to the child.
- ☐ I feel angry.
- ☐ I wonder what the child might be thinking.
- ☐ I'd rather not look at the picture.
- ☐ I feel guilty.
- ☐ I feel responsible to a certain extent.

2 🔊 Listen and react

The fact that children in developing countries are suffering from the effects of hard and often dangerous work is generally known to most of us. Listen to the text with books closed. What words cross your mind when you hear it? Share your ideas in small groups.

3 Read and put meaning into words

In your group, choose words from the text you relate to hazardous child labour and complete the mind map with them. Share your results in class.

The world should, indeed,
    have outgrown the intolerable forms
    of abuse and exploitation
    the poor and disadvantaged
    labouring children endure.
    But it hasn't.

The world ought to, indeed,
    regard any kind of child labour
    as something unjustifiable.
    And instead should truly respect
    the children's human rights.
    But it doesn't.

The world should not, indeed,
    tolerate the exploitation of poverty.
    Protection from hazardous labour
    should be a right for all the children
    living in this world.
    But it isn't.

The world, indeed, will have to
    urgently improve education.
    For knowledge and practical skills
    can enable these desperate children
    to improve their situation and lives.
    Let's hope it will.

4 🔊 Listen and discuss

Interviews with working children in developing countries have shown that a large majority would like to attend school and have clear ideas about the value of education. While listening to a radio programme, add more words to the mind map. Compare and recall the facts.

5 Discuss and use these expressions

How many children work world-wide? How many can't attend school and why, do you think? Which parts of the world are most affected by a lack of education? Share your ideas, expressing ignorance and certainty. Use the expressions on the right. Finally, compare your ideas with the charts on page 79.

I couldn't say. / I couldn't tell you.
I've no idea, I'm afraid.
I haven't the slightest idea.

There's no doubt about ...
I'm quite certain that ...
Everybody knows that ...

6 Discuss, write and read

Before you read each of the following extracts, discuss every preceding statement (a) in small groups.
Then find an additional argument (b). Compare your suggestions at the end.

Hidden exploitation

Child labour mainly happens
a) in developing countries.

b) ....
While the vast majority of working children are found in developing countries, children routinely work in all countries. Few people in the industrialised world, for example, would look upon the employment of a child to deliver newspapers for an hour or two before school as an exploitative form of child labour, despite the fact that the child will be paid very little for it. Children in developing countries, however, don't have the power of free choice. Not only are they pushed into work, but they are forced to do work that is often damaging to their development and health.

Industrialised countries almost universally accept that if children are to develop normally and healthily, then they are not supposed to
a) do disabling work.

b) ....
In the early decades of industrialisation, work was thought to be the most effective way of teaching children about life, whereas today, education, play and leisure, friends, good health and proper rest must all have an important place in children's lives. In contrast to this, a high proportion of child employees in developing countries are expected to give their entire wages to their parents. Without the income of working children aged 13-17, poverty would rise by between 10 and 20 per cent.

Child labour will never be eliminated until
a) poverty disappears completely.

b) ....
It is true that the poorest, most disadvantaged sectors of society supply the vast majority of child labourers. But, however poor their families may be, children would not be harmed by work if there were not people prepared and able to exploit them. There is no doubt that whenever a child is engaged in hazardous labour, someone – an employer, a customer or a parent – benefits from that labour. It is this element of exploitation that is overlooked by those who see child labour as inseparable from poverty. As good quality education is believed to keep children away from damaging child labour, the fight must begin with relevant educational programmes which children will want to participate in.

41

Language in action

1 Exchange information

How are people like politicians, film stars, sport celebrities generally seen by the public? What do we tend to say about them? Think of some names. Or how do people see you? Is it true what they sometimes say about you? Share your ideas in small groups, using these expressions:

He/She is / I'm   said to ... / considered to ...
                   known to ... / believed to ...

e.g. *I'm said to have a lot of patience. – I suppose I have.*

2 Read and share your ideas

Read the situations below. In small groups, discuss what each member will probably choose to do in every situation and give reasons, like this:
Sarah will probably choose to work in a developing country as she loves helping people. She most probably won't go to Greece or Alaska. Since she is a very active person she will presumably join a walking tour in Scotland.

1 You have been offered two jobs: as a managing director of an important company and as head of a team working on a project in a developing country.
2 There are three last-minute offers available for your two-week summer holiday: a package tour to the island of Rhodes in Greece, a cruise to Alaska or a walking tour in Scotland.
3 You have won a prize in a raffle. You can choose between an art book, a coffee machine, a CD with pop music and a travel bag.
4 You have a week of absolute freedom and there are no duties, family or other commitments to consider. You can choose to do whatever you feel like.
5 It is Saturday and you have been invited to a party by a good friend, to a concert by another and to a lovely dinner at the Hilton by yet another friend for the same evening.

3 Make your choice and find out

Work with a partner and choose one of the people on the picture page of Topic 3, p. 19. Imagine and, if you like, write down what this person will do, will be doing or will have done in five years' time. Then, sit in groups of four and ask another pair questions to find out which person they have chosen, like this:
– *Will the person buy an expensive car in five years time?*
– *Will he or she still be living in the same place?*
– *Will he or she have changed his or her job?*

4 Write and use these expressions

What will have changed by the year 2030, do you think? Where and how will people be living, working and spending their free time? Look at the headlines below and use your imagination. In small groups, write down some assumptions using these expressions:
It's very likely/unlikely that ...
We strongly believe that ...
Presumably/Probably ...

e.g. *It's very likely that pupils will be learning and doing exams by computer only. Presumably schools will have closed by the year 2030.*

Abandoned Schools
Home cinema alive   **A new Start at 80**   **Cash is out**
MOON HOTEL FULLY BOOKED
No more commuting   **Single for Life**

Highways for inline skaters

5 Discuss and make your point

Compare your assumptions about the headlines and make some conclusions, like this:
Supposing pupils will be learning by computer only, they will probably miss their friends.

6 Exchange information and find out

Try to remember how long you will have been doing, or you will have done, something by the end of this year and write down the number of years or months only. Then exchange your notes with a partner, who tries to find out what you are thinking of. Say 'right' or 'wrong' only. These key words might help you: town, house, flat, marriage, car, bicycle, sports, work, fitness, hobby, computer.
Here's an example: 7   5   9   16
– *By the end of this year, you will have been working in your company for 7 years.*
– *I'm afraid, you're wrong.*
– *You will have had your bicycle for 7 years.*
– *That's right.*

Activity reading

1 Tune in

Cat in the rain is a short story by Ernest Hemingway. He was born in 1898 in a highly respectable suburb of Chicago, where his father was a doctor. He was the second of six children. He worked as a reporter, volunteered as an ambulance driver on the Italian front where he was badly wounded; he later came to Europe as a roving correspondent and visited Spain during the Civil War. He gradually took to a life that admired bull-fighting, big-game hunting and deep-sea fishing. Early in life, he established himself as the master of a new, tough, and peculiarly American style of writing and became a legend during his lifetime. In 1954 he was awarded a Nobel Prize for Literature. He died in Cuba in July 1961.
⇨ Cultural information, p. 80

2 🔊)) Read or listen and discuss

Read or listen to the beginning of the story and in small groups speculate on the following questions. Share your ideas in class.
1 What kind of place does the author describe in the text?
2 What season is it?
3 What's the atmosphere like?
4 What kind of story is going to take place here?

Use these expressions to express assumptions:
It looks/seems as if …
Probably/Presumably …
We have the feeling that …

Cat in the rain

There were only two Americans stopping at the hotel. They did not know any of the people they passed on the stairs on their way to and from their room. Their room was on the second floor facing the sea. It also faced the public garden and the war monument. There were big palms and green benches in the public garden. In the good weather there was always an artist with his easel. Artists liked the way the palms grew and the bright colours of the hotels facing the gardens and the sea. Italians came from a long way off to look up at the war monument. It was made of bronze and glistened in the rain. It was raining. The rain dripped from the palm trees. Water stood in pools on the gravel paths. The sea broke in a long line in the rain and slipped back down the beach to come up and break again in a long line in the rain.

The motor-cars were gone from the square by the war monument. Across the square in the doorway of the café a waiter stood looking out at the empty square.

3 Read and exchange information

Now, find out more about the people involved, their relationship and their actions in the story. Divide the class into two groups, group A and B.
Group A read the extracts on page 75, group B turn to page 76. Read the instructions and the extracts carefully. Once you have completed your task, form A/B-pairs and compare your answers to these questions with the help of your notes.

1 What kind of room is it?
2 What's the atmosphere in the room like?
3 What's the relationship between the two characters? Do they like each other?
4 In what way do the two people differ in personality?
5 Is there a problem? If yes, what kind of problem is it?
6 What are their individual needs?
Finally, read the complete story on pages 44 - 45.

Cat in the rain

by Ernest Hemingway

There were only two Americans stopping at the hotel...

The American wife stood at the window looking out. Outside right under their window a cat was crouched under one of the dripping green tables. The cat was trying to make herself so compact that she would not be dripped on.

"I'm going down and get that kitty," the American wife said.

"I'll do it," her husband offered from the bed.

"No, I'll get it. The poor kitty out trying to keep dry under a table."

The husband went on reading, lying propped up with the two pillows at the foot of the bed.

"Don't get wet," he said.

The wife went downstairs and the hotel owner stood up and bowed to her as she passed the office. His desk was at the far end of the office. He was an old man and very tall.

"*Il piove*," the wife said. She liked the hotel-keeper.

"*Si, si, Signora, brutto tempo*. It is very bad weather."

He stood behind his desk in the far end of the dim room. The wife liked him. She liked the deadly serious way he received any complaints. She liked his dignity. She liked the way he wanted to serve her. She liked the way he felt about being a hotel-keeper. She liked his old, heavy face and big hands.

Liking him she opened the door and looked out. It was raining harder. A man in a rubber cape was crossing the empty square to the café. The cat would be around to the right. Perhaps she could go along under the eaves. As she stood in the doorway an umbrella opened behind her. It was the maid who looked after their room.

"You must not get wet," she smiled, speaking Italian. Of course, the hotel-keeper had sent her.

With the maid holding the umbrella over her, she walked along the gravel path until she was under their window. The table was there, washed bright green in the rain, but the cat was gone. She was suddenly disappointed. The maid looked up at her.

"*Ha perduto qualque cosa, Signora?*"

"There was a cat," said the American girl.

"A cat?"

"*Si, il gatto.*"

"A cat?" the maid laughed. "A cat in the rain?"

"Yes," she said, "under the table." Then, "Oh, I wanted it so much. I wanted a kitty."

When she talked English the maid's face tightened.

"Come, Signora," she said. "We must get back inside. You will be wet."

"I suppose so," said the American girl.

They went back along the gravel path and passed the door. The maid stayed outside to close the umbrella. As the American girl passed the office, the *padrone* bowed from his desk. Something felt very small and tight inside the girl. The *padrone* made her feel very small and at the same time really important. She had a momentary feeling of being of supreme importance. She went on up the stairs. She opened the door of the room. George was on the bed, reading.

"Did you get the cat?" he asked, putting the book down.

"It was gone."

"Wonder where it went to?" he said, resting his eyes from reading.

She sat down on the bed.

"I wanted it so much," she said. "I don't know why I wanted it so much. I wanted that poor kitty. It isn't any fun to be a poor kitty out in the rain."

George was reading again.

She went over and sat in front of the mirror of the dressing table, looking at herself with the hand glass. She studied her profile, first one side and then the other. Then she studied the back of her head and her neck.

"Don't you think it would be a good idea if I let my hair grow out?" she asked, looking at her profile again.

George looked up and saw the back of her neck, clipped close like a boy's.

"I like it the way it is."

"I get so tired of it," she said. "I get so tired of looking like a boy."

George shifted his position on the bed. He hadn't looked away from her since she started to speak.

"You look pretty darn nice," he said.

She laid the mirror down on the dresser and went over to the window and looked out. It was getting dark.

"I want to pull my hair back tight and smooth and make a big knot at the back that I can feel," she said. "I want to have a kitty to sit on my lap and purr when I stroke her."

"Yeah?" George said from the bed.

"And I want to eat at a table with my own silver and I want candles. And I want it to be spring and I want to brush my hair out in front of a mirror and I want a kitty and I want some new clothes."

"Oh, shut up and get something to read," George said. He was reading again.

His wife was looking out of the window. It was quite dark now and still raining in the palm trees.

"Anyway, I want a cat," she said. "I want a cat. I want a cat now. If I can't have long hair or any fun, I can have a cat."

George was not listening. He was reading his book. His wife looked out of the window where the light had come on in the square.

Someone knocked at the door.

"*Avanti,*" George said. He looked up from his book.

In the doorway stood the maid. She held a big tortoiseshell cat pressed tight against her and swung down against her body.

"Excuse me," she said, "the *padrone* asked me to bring this for the Signora."

Activity reading

1 Tune in
An aborigine is a member of the group of people that have lived in Australia from the earliest times. What do you know about the Australian aborigines? Share your ideas in groups and then in class.
➪ Cultural information, p. 80

2 Discuss and share your ideas
What might the woman in the picture on the right have experienced in her life? Has she suffered a lot, do you think? What are the difficulties she has had to struggle with? Don't read the poem yet, but look at the following words. What do they tell you about her life? Answer the questions in small groups.
wedded, enslaved, whitewashed, shaped, scolded, cursed, damned, labelled.

Maureen Watson

3 🔊 Listen and find out
Listen to the poem with books closed. Then, try to find some answers to these questions.
1 What has this woman missed in her life?
2 What does she call her personal achievements?
3 What does personal value mean to her?

4 Read and make your point
In small groups, discuss the answers to the questions above in more detail and take notes. Then, underline or copy the parts of the poem you find most impressive and thought-provoking. Share your thoughts in class later.

STEPPING OUT
by Maureen Watson

I'm stepping out, don't mess about.
Don't tell me to be patient,
I've been wedded, enslaved, whitewashed, and saved,
But now, I'm liberated.
I've been patted, and moulded, and shaped, and scolded
And I learned real fast how to please 'em,
I "yessir"ed, and "No ma'am"ed,
I was cursed and damned,
And all for no good reason.
I've been put up, and I've been put down,
By folks who were black, white, yellow or brown,
Treated like I wasn't human, just a puppet, a token,
But I healed my hurts, 'cause for better or worse,
Black woman's got spirit that's never going to be broken.
Been labelled all my life,
Black woman, mother and wife.
And their labels formed the bars of my prison,
But I've got to set free, this person who's me,
'cause now I've got a vision.
Their myths and lies are dead,
Not heaped on my head,
And their history is all outdated,
Different sex, different skin, can't change what's within,
'cause now, I'm liberated.
And I'm stepping out, don't mess about,
Don't tell me to be patient,
No ifs or buts.
I don't walk, I strut,
'cause now, I'm liberated.

5 Discuss and write

Do you remember Jane who suddenly was obsessed by a need to learn? With a partner or individually, write a short poem Jane might have written. If you like, use these phrases.

I'm stepping out,
Don't tell me to ...
I've been ...
But now, I'm ...
And I learnt ...

Activity reading

1 Tune in

What title or message do you think the artist of this statue had in mind? Does it attract people's attention? Why?/Why not? Discuss in small groups and share your ideas in class.

2 Discuss and make your point

The number of people living alone is increasing. But the so-called 'singles' have changed compared to the former 'bachelors'. What's the advantage of living alone? What do these statements tell us about the life of a single person? Discuss in groups.

1 Singles regard their friends as their family.
2 The main problem for single people is to find another single person to go on holiday with.
3 In cases of desperation, single women team up together to go to health farms.
4 No single female is ever content with the direction of her career.
5 Godchildren are the most fashionable accessory for single people.
6 Single females constantly and secretly wonder if they will ever marry.

3 Discuss and write

The following questions give you some hints about the story. What do you expect to happen? What other questions enter your mind? With a partner, write down some more and share your ideas in class.

1 How did Mrs Mallard react to the bad news?
2 To what extent did the time of the year reflect her feelings?
3 What kind of life had she had until then?
4 What did she imagine life to be like in the future?
5 Could you describe Mrs Mallard and her husband?
6 Why might the story also be called 'The Dream of an Hour'?

Now read these extracts and answer the questions above as far as possible.

The Story of an Hour

She could see in the open square before her house the tops of trees that were all slightly trembling with the new spring life. The delicious breath of rain was in the air. (...) The notes of a distant song which someone was singing reached her faintly, and countless sparrows were twittering in the eaves. (...) But now there was a dull stare in her eyes, whose gaze was fixed away off on one of those patches of blue sky.

(...)

When she abandoned herself a little whispered word escaped her slightly parted lips. She said it over and over under her breath: "free, free, free!" The vacant stare and the look of terror that had followed it went from her eyes.

(...)

But she saw beyond that bitter moment a long procession of years to come that would belong to her absolutely. And she opened and spread her arms out to them in welcome.

There would be no one to live for her during those coming years; she would live for herself. There would be no powerful will bending hers in that blind persistence with which men and women believe they have a right to impose a private will upon a fellow-creature.

(...)

She breathed a quick prayer that life might be long. It was only yesterday she had thought with a shudder that life might be long.

4 🔊 Listen and react

Listen to the beginning of the story with books closed. Then, try to answer the questions 1-6 and your own questions from task 3 again. Finally, read the whole story.

The Story of an Hour

by Kate Chopin (1851-1904)

⇨ Cultural information, p. 80

Knowing that Mrs Mallard was afflicted with a heart trouble, great care was taken to break to her as gently as possible the news of her husband's death.

It was her sister Josephine who told her, in broken sentences. Her husband's friend Richards was there, too, near her. It was he who had been in the newspaper office when intelligence of the railroad disaster was received, with Brently Mallard's name leading the list of 'killed'. He had only taken the time to assure himself of its truth by a second telegram, and had hastened to carefully pass on the sad message to his tender friend.

She did not hear the story as many women have heard the same, with a paralyzed inability to accept its significance. She wept at once, with sudden, wild abandonment, in her sister's arms. When the storm of grief had spent itself she went away to her room alone. She would have no one follow her.

There stood, facing the open window, a comfortable, roomy armchair. Into this she sank, pressed down by a physical exhaustion that haunted her body and seemed to reach into her soul.

She could see in the open square before her house the tops of trees that were all slightly trembling with the new spring life. The delicious breath of rain was in the air. In the street below a peddler was crying his wares. The notes of a distant song which someone was singing reached her faintly, and countless sparrows were twittering in the eaves.

There were patches of blue sky showing here and there through the clouds that had met and piled one above the other in the west facing her window.

She sat with her head thrown back upon the cushion of the chair, quite motionless, except when a sob came up into her throat and shook her, as a child who has cried itself to sleep continues to sob in its dreams.

She was young, with a fair, calm face, whose lines bespoke repression and even a certain strength. But now there was a dull stare in her eyes, whose gaze was fixed away off on one of those patches of blue sky. It was not a glance of reflection, but rather indicated a suspension of intelligent thought.

There was something coming to her and she was waiting for it, fearfully. What was it? She did not know; it was too subtle and difficult to name. But she felt it, creeping out of the sky, reaching toward her through the sounds, the scents, the color that filled the air.

Now her bosom rose and fell tumultuously. She was beginning to recognize this thing that was approaching to possess her, and she was striving to beat it back with her will – as powerless as her two white slender hands would have been.

When she abandoned herself a little whispered word escaped her slightly parted lips. She said it over and over under her breath: "free, free, free!" The vacant stare and the look of terror that had

followed it went from her eyes. They stayed keen and bright. Her pulses beat fast, and the coursing blood warmed and relaxed every inch of her body.

She did not stop to ask if it were or were not a monstrous joy that held her. A clear and joyful perception enabled her to treat the suggestion as trivial.

She knew that she would weep again when she saw the kind, tender hands folded in death; the face that had never looked save with love upon her, fixed and gray and dead. But she saw beyond that bitter moment a long procession of years to come that would belong to her absolutely. And she opened and spread her arms out to them in welcome.

There would be no one to live for her during those coming years; she would live for herself. There would be no powerful will bending hers in that blind persistence with which men and women believe they have a right to impose a private will upon a fellow-creature. A kind intention or a cruel intention made the act seem no less a crime as she looked upon it in that brief moment of illumination.

And yet she had loved him – sometimes. Often she had not. What did it matter! What could love, the unsolved mystery, count for in face of this possession of self-assertion which she suddenly recognized as the strongest impulse of her being!

"Free! Body and soul free!" she kept whispering.

Josephine was kneeling before the closed door with her lips to the keyhole, begging for admission. "Louise, open the door! I beg; open the door – you will make yourself ill. What are you doing, Louise? For heaven's sake open the door."

"Go away, I am not making myself ill." No, she was drinking in a very elixir of life through that open widow.

Her fancy was running riot along those days ahead of her. Spring days, and summer days, and all sorts of days that would be her own. She breathed a quick prayer that life might be long. It was only yesterday she had thought with a shudder that life might be long.

She arose at length and opened the door to her sister's demand. There was a feverish triumph in her eyes, and she carried herself unwittingly like a goddess of Victory. She clasped her sister's waist, and together they descended the stairs. Richards stood waiting for them at the bottom.

Someone was opening the front door with a latchkey. It was Brently Mallard who entered, a little travel-stained, calmly carrying his grip-sack and umbrella. He had been far from the scene of accident, and did not even know there had been one. He stood amazed at Josephine's piercing cry; at Richards' quick motion to cover him from the view of his wife.

But Richards was too late.

When the doctors came they said she had died of heart disease – of joy that kills.

Activity reading

4

51

1 Tune in

Have you ever spent a holiday together with some friends or another family? Perhaps you rented a house or organised a trip together. Was it an experience you would want to repeat? Which of the following aspects would you consider relevant before you decide to share a holiday with somebody? Number them according to importance. Add more if you like. Then talk to a partner and give reasons.

☐ behaviour ☐ manners ☐ age ☐ habits ☐ preferences ☐ responsibility ☐ money

2 Read and find out

Here's the beginning and ending of a story which although funny, is unbelievably realistic. Read both parts. What do you think might have happened in between? Discuss in small groups and take some notes to share in class later.

The holiday friends from hell

David and I had always longed to rent one of those magnificent farmhouses in the Italian countryside, and used to spend many happy evenings staring at photographs in brochures. The idea of such peace and quiet, with a swimming pool thrown in, seemed like heaven on earth.

There was, however, just one problem: the cost. Almost all the houses we looked at were vast and clearly designed for groups, rather than couples. They were also hideously expensive, which was why we hit on the idea of asking another couple, Emma and Richard, to share the burden.

We had known Richard for years, and it seemed a brilliant plan to invite him and his girlfriend along. So we were delighted when, after seeing a tempting picture of the villa, they agreed straight away.

The four of us flew out together, and picked up a car in Pisa. From there it was a short drive to the place where we were to spend a whole delicious fortnight. I was looking forward to every single sun-kissed minute. Little did I know what lay in store.

... ? ...

At Heathrow, with a collective inward sigh of relief, we went our separate ways. "Thank you so much for organising the trip," said Emma, in an icy voice. "We so enjoyed ourselves." At her side, a still lobster-red Richard nodded vigorously. They sent us a card with a message to the same effect some time afterwards, although it was quite obvious how they really felt.

3 🔊 Read or listen and discuss

Now read or listen to the main part of the story. Stop after every paragraph and each time answer the following questions in small groups and take some notes. Before you go on, share your ideas in class.

1 How would you have felt in this situation?
2 How would you have reacted?
3 What would you have said to any of the people involved?

The holiday friends from hell

... Little did I know what lay in store.

On the first morning, I was sitting on the terrace by the pool, drinking my coffee when I had the most terrible shock. I had never seen Richard, who is rather plump, in any state of undress before, yet there he was, resplendent before me in the smallest pair of swimming trunks I have ever seen. I felt myself go a deep shade of red.

Unfortunately, his way of dressing was something I had to get used to over the next fourteen days. If we were going out to eat, he would just throw a shirt over his bulging frame. He seemed to delight in flashing his body at us. Sometimes it was a struggle to force my pasta down with him parading around the place.

Worse still, as the days went by, his pasty skin got more and more burnt. By the end of the first week, he was bright red. He looked like one of the exotic salamis we had seen hanging up at the market. Not that he was bothered. "Isn't my tan great?" he'd say, stroking his deep red arms.

◆

The kitchen in the house was fantastic, so we agreed that each couple would take it in turns to cook dinner. It was our turn first. We started off with air-dried ham, followed by veal, with lots of fruit and delicious cheeses afterwards. Next, it was their turn. They gave us weedy asparagus, followed by a rather poor salad. So, the following evening, we dished up roast chicken and zabaglione, hoping they'd take the hint. Alas, the following evening, they produced tuna and sweetcorn sandwiches.

Mealtimes went on like this for the whole holiday. Worse still, whenever we went out to eat, they would always argue about the bill. (...)

◆

At the beginning of week two, David and I were sitting outside in the cool of the evening having a quiet drink. Emma and Richard had already made their excuses and gone up to bed — a place where they seemed to spend a great deal of time. Unfortunately, their room was at the front of the house, and as we sipped our wine, we found we could hear every word they said through the open windows. It quickly became apparent — to my horror — that Richard and Emma had nicknames for us.

"Don't you find it weird that Catweazle insists on having Weetabix, even though it's twice the price here than it is at home?" said Richard, obviously referring to David.

"Yes," replied Emma, "I suppose it is rather annoying, but not half as irritating as Jamjar's obsession with hygiene." Then the pair of them collapsed into giggles. We still have no idea what these names meant.

◆

But the worst came about three nights before we were due to leave. Richard had decided that the holiday was not going with a swing because we weren't drinking enough. He accused us of being squares and announced that he was off into town to "get in the beers". That night, he insisted we were going to get well and truly smashed.

After a thoroughly alcohol-drenched dinner — some kind of indeterminate pasta — Richard yelled delightedly and finally jumped into the swimming pool, almost drowning. David fortunately was quick and sober enough to save him and help him out of the pool. After this incident, there was a terrible silence. Then Emma stood up, "You bastard. Good-night everyone," she said and stormed inside.

◆

The remaining three days of the holiday we had so looked forward to were punctuated by Richard and Emma's rows, which seemed to break out every time we left the room. The rest of the time, she sulked.

◆

(...) They sent us a card with a message to the same effect some time afterwards, although it was quite obvious how they really felt.

Activity reading

5

1 Tune in

How do you see the future society? Choose any of the following words which you spontaneously relate to this topic. Then decide whether you consider the development of the issues to be positive (+) or negative (-) and mark each box accordingly. Later, compare your results in small groups.

- ☐ communication
- ☐ relationships
- ☐ discrimination
- ☐ achievements
- ☐ discoveries
- ☐ technology
- ☐ living standards
- ☐ human rights
- ☐ social security
- ☐ satisfaction
- ☐ progress
- ☐ security
- ☐ nutrition
- ☐ waste
- ☐ space
- ☐ justice
- ☐ challenge
- ☐ power
- ☐ politics
- ☐ peace
- ☐ medicine
- ☐ work
- ☐ research
- ☐ energy
- ☐ religion
- ☐ happiness
- ☐ family
- ☐ population
- ☐ education
- ☐ pollution

2 Discuss and share your ideas

Choose the ten most important words from the list above which you would want your future society to consider most. In a group, argue and give reasons for your personal choice. Once your group has agreed on ten words, draw a huge flag, adding any lines, shapes or even colours to it. Then discuss and place your words anywhere in the flag according to their importance. Finally, show and describe your flag to the class giving reasons for your choices.

3 Discuss and make your point

Imagine we had a World State and its flag was decorated with these three words:

Community   Identity   Stability

How would you value a World State where priorities were expressed by these words? What do they mean in regard to its aims, ideas and rules? What would its society and life be like, do you think? Discuss in your group and then share your ideas.

4 Read and discuss

In the first chapter of A. Huxley's book **Brave New World** we can find the description below. Read and with a partner discuss the advantages (if any) and disadvantages of this philosophy. Is it fiction or fact?

Brave New World

Over the main door was the World State's motto: Community, Identity, Stability. Those three words expressed the World State's political programme. By community, the World State meant that its citizens must live at peace with each other. They must live only to serve the State. By identity, the World State meant that everybody in each social group must be exactly like everybody else in that group. They must not try to be different. Indeed, after their training and education – their 'conditioning' – they would not have the power to be different. By stability, the World State meant that its citizens must be contented and obedient. They must not try to change society in any way. The World State knew what was best for everybody.

⇨ Cultural information, p. 81

5 Read and write

The following headlines appeared in different newspapers. Can you think of any others you could imagine finding in future newspapers? Discuss in small groups and write them down. To what extent do they relate to the text above?

Donor eggs
Human Fertilisation
Genetic programming to create a baby
Frozen embryos destroyed after five years in storage

6 🔊 Listen and discuss

Now, listen to the beginning of Chapter 1 with books closed. How close to reality is Huxley's prediction? Discuss. Finally, read the whole chapter.

Brave New World

by Aldous Huxley

Chapter One

A low grey building. Low for those times. Yet it contained thirty-four floors. Over the main door were the words: CENTRAL LONDON HATCHERY AND CONDITIONING CENTRE.

Here, human eggs were brought to birth – or 'hatched' – by scientists. Children were produced from those eggs. That was the meaning of HATCHERY.

Here, too, the human eggs were treated by scientists. The eggs were made clever or stupid or average. They were made tall or short. Then the children that came out of the eggs were trained and educated. They received the training and education for their particular social class or group. The World State decided what sort of people they should become. That was the meaning of CONDITIONING.

Over the main door, too, was the World State's motto: COMMUNITY, IDENTITY, STABILITY. Those three words expressed the World State's political programme.

By COMMUNITY, the World State meant that its citizens must live at peace with each other. They must live only to serve the State.

By IDENTITY, the World State meant that everybody in each social group must be exactly like everybody else in that group. They must not try to be different. Indeed, after their training and education – their 'conditioning' – they would not have the power to be different.

By STABILITY, the World State meant that its citizens must be contented and obedient. They must not try to change society in any way. The World State knew what was best for everybody.

The very big room on the lowest floor looked north. It was cold. The scientists wore white coats. They had dead-coloured rubber gloves on their hands. The light was frozen and dead. Only the yellow barrels of the microscopes shone. On work table after work table, the light lay on those polished tubes as yellow as butter.

'And this,' said the Director, opening the door, 'is the Fertilising Room. This is where life is given to the human eggs.'

Three hundred Fertilisers – the scientists who brought the eggs to life – were bending over their instruments. An anxious band of new students followed the Director. They wrote all his words in their notebooks. The Director of Hatcheries and Conditioning for Central London always took his new students round the Centre. He gave them a general idea of how it worked. They needed a general idea in order to do their special work well. Tomorrow, they would start on their special work. Special work and particular ideas made it easy to fit people into the social system. Everybody in the World State did the special work and had the particular ideas for which he had been *conditioned*.

Tall and rather thin, but upright, the Director advanced into the Fertilising Room. Old? Young? Thirty? Fifty? Fifty-five? It was hard to say. Anyhow, nobody asked. In this year of *Stability* – After Ford 632 – human beings, like everything else, changed very little.

'I shall begin at the beginning,' said the D.H.C. Some students wrote even that down: *Begin at the beginning*. 'These,' he waved his hand, 'are the incubators.' He pointed to the glass tubes in which life was given to the eggs. Mixed together in a warm liquid, male seed and female eggs joined. Children were produced like this. They did not have fathers or mothers or homes. They were brought to life in the World State Hatcheries. They were brought up in the World State Nurseries.

The Director reminded the students that men and women gave the Centre male seed and female eggs. They did this for the sake of the Social System. They were rewarded for it, too.

After being examined under powerful microscopes, the fertilised eggs were divided

into five groups. Those in the top group were called Alphas. Then came the Betas. Then the Gammas. Then the Deltas. Then the Epsilons.

The Alphas and Betas were left to grow in the warm liquid. The Gammas, Deltas and Epsilons were treated with X-rays and drugs. The eggs in these low groups multiplied to provide the World State with its less educated servants. They looked after the machines in the factories and carried out other necessary work. They did not need to be clever to do their work. The Fertilisers in the Centre could produce as many as ninety-six Gammas or Deltas or Epsilons from a single egg. Each of them would look and feel and think exactly like all the others in the group.

'This is progress,' said the Director. 'The discovery of how to control birth and produce people like machines is the cause of our social stability. Nobody thinks of making changes. Nobody wants to make changes. We plan human beings and then we match them to their future employment.'

The Alphas and Betas were also trained to be obedient servants of the World State. But as future managers, directors and highly-skilled workers, they were also trained to be clever. They were few in number compared with the other groups.

The Director was now joined by Henry Foster, a yellow-haired, healthy-looking young man. Mr Foster explained the work of the Conditioning Department at the Centre. This was a big laboratory in which the growing human eggs received the minds and bodies that the World State decided to give them.

The State knew how many Alphas, Betas, Gammas, Deltas and Epsilons it wanted. It knew, in other words, how many clever and how many stupid people it needed. The Conditioning Departments in Hatcheries in all parts of the world produced the right numbers in each group.

'We produce our babies,' Mr Foster said, 'as socialised human beings. They are grown here as Epsilons or Alphas. We produce them as we need them – Betas, Gammas, Deltas, too. We produce them to be future factory workers, future Fertilisers, or future Directors of Hatcheries. Epsilons,' he explained, 'don't need human intelligence. They are as stupid as animals. But they must be made ready for their work as quickly as possible. The other groups are given the intelligence – the cleverness – they need. Then all are trained to do their work and to like it.'

The students then learned how X-rays and drugs and liquid food were given to the growing eggs. They saw how the eggs were conditioned. Future workers in hot countries were trained to enjoy heat. Future space engineers were trained to enjoy being head over heels. This training was called 'Condition-ing'. Through conditioning, the eggs were being prepared for their future work. Through conditioning, the eggs were being prepared for their future social rank. Conditioning made them happy and obedient.

'That,' said the Director, 'is the secret of happiness and virtue. We make people like what they have *got* to do. All our training aims at that. We condition our babies and our children to like a social future from which they cannot escape.'

It was now time to go up to the Nurseries where the children were trained.

6 ▶ Activity reading

1 Tune in

Imagine you found these two pictures in a magazine. What headline would you give an article accompanying both pictures? What could the article be about? Discuss in small groups and then share your ideas.

2 Read and exchange information

There are two main characters in the story that follows. It takes place in London and reflects the relationship between a man and a woman. Divide the class into two groups. Group A read the text on page 76, group B turn to page 78. Work with a partner from your group and answer the questions listed. Make individual notes. When everybody is ready, form A/B pairs and compare the two characters by reporting your answers.

3 Share your ideas and use these expressions

Discuss the questions below in class. Use these phrases in order to express doubt:
I rather doubt whether …
I'm not so certain about …
I might be wrong, but …
From what I've read I'd say that …

1 What do Bob and Sharon have in common? In what ways are they different?
2 What do they both lack?
3 What are their prospects? Who can survive more easily?
4 What's their relationship in the story, do you think?

4 🔊 Read or listen and make your point

Here's the beginning of the story. Once you have read or listened to it, answer the questions above again in class. Then with a partner, write down a few questions expressing your curiosity and interest in the facts given. Discuss and speculate on some answers.

The comfort of strangers

Bob Easton was half asleep the first time he saw her. He was lying in the doorway of the Vaudeville Theatre on the Strand, well wrapped up in his sleeping bag and his blankets, and on an ordinary night he would probably have been fast asleep by now. But it was Friday, the worst night of the week on the streets, when you're more likely than ever to get a kick in the ribs from some lager lover, so Bob Easton had one eye open for trouble, which is how he came to spot Sharon.

She looked completely lost, wandering along the Strand in the dark with a little black jacket pulled tight around her top. He could tell she was young and there was something about the way she moved that made Bob think she was worried. He had seen the kind of trouble these young people could get into, so he caught her eye and she trotted straight over and told him she had nowhere to go. "I'm scared," she said.

"I'm not bloody surprised you're scared," muttered Bob.

And when she asked if she could come in there with him, he said that was all right, if that's what she wanted, and so she ducked into his doorway, slipped into his pile of bedding, pulled a couple of blankets over her head and told him not to let anyone know she was there.

The comfort of strangers

... Sharon was soon asleep, but Bob Easton lay awake for a while, checking the passersby and wondering whether this was altogether a good idea. (...)

And when he woke up early the next morning and found that she was still with him, he wondered a little more. She was a cheerful little thing in the daylight, but she was pretty guarded when it came to talking about herself. She said her name was Sharon Gibson. Bob very much doubted that. The streets were full of people who were hiding from something, covering their tracks with dodgy names. She told him she was 18 but, to his eye, she looked a fair bit younger, which worried him, because a young girl on the streets is nothing but trouble.

(...) She was in a complete mess. It seemed she had been living rough for some time and she had broken up with some bloke and she had been messing around with drugs, too. Bob wondered if it could have been some dealer that had made her get so frightened the night before. She had no money at all and the only possession she seemed to care about was her little black jacket. She said she begged a lot. Then she admitted she had been working round King's Cross, selling herself for twenty pounds. Bob shook his head and decided he had better break his own rules, just for the morning. "Come along with me," he said.

At that moment, he was still thinking it would be simple. He'd take her along to the DSS[1] office in Chadwick Street, he would get her to sign on, she'd get some money and that would keep her away from the punters and the dealers while she sorted herself out. And then he'd go back to his doorway alone. He sat in the waiting area at the DSS and watched while she gave her details to the counter clerk and, within minutes, he could see his plan falling apart. The clerk sent her round the corner to Youth Employment. Bob knew the DSS — in a former life he had worked for them for 14 years — and if they were sending her to Youth Employment, it meant she was under 18 and they wouldn't give her a penny.

The two of them walked away empty-handed. Bob had no idea what to do now. He didn't see how he could abandon her. She was just a child, wandering along with no idea of how bad the fall would be if she put a foot wrong. But he didn't want her. She'd mess up his life and, anyway, he had never been too good at being close with people.

(...) But then again, this Sharon was very pleasant in her way, he thought. Perhaps it wouldn't hurt to try and help her a little more.

For three or four weeks, it went well. Bob had a bright idea and got her selling the Big Issue[2]. By day, they'd haunt the pavements of the Strand, selling the magazine, stopping now and then for a cup of tea or a cake, and by night they'd bed down in their doorway together. There was no sex in this. He was at least 30 years older than her. It was more father and daughter, and Bob was quite proud of her. Sometimes they'd split the work and she'd take one side of the street while he worked the other, and she'd always come back and give him everything she'd earned, so they could divide it between them. She was not taking drugs. She never went near King's Cross. The truth was, he had started to enjoy having her around. Then the boyfriend came back.

He was a punk called Mick with tattoos on his arms and a bright yellow slash running through his hair. Sharon had told Bob a bit about him, how she'd met him on the streets and they'd started spending all their time together, with her doing some begging and him selling hot dogs from a stand in Covent Garden, and then how

---

[1] DSS = Department of Social Security. The British government department which is responsible for paying people benefits, e.g. family credit or unemployment benefit.

[2] The Big Issue = Special magazine with articles written by people who are living on the streets of Britain and sold to anybody interested. It helps street people to make some money.

⇨ Cultural information, p. 81

they'd split up. Bob had forgotten all about him but now suddenly here he was. Bob watched him talking to Sharon and saw her come across to him and heard her say she wanted to go off with him. "Is that all right?" she asked.

"Course it is," said Bob, who tended to talk down at his feet when he was shy. "I'm just looking after you. We're not following each other around the streets."

That night, for the first time in nearly a month, Bob slept alone on the steps of the Vaudeville Theatre. It didn't feel good. He was not about to say he missed her, whatever the truth might be, but he knew very well that he was worried about her. (...)

When days passed with no sign of Sharon, Bob couldn't stand it. He hid his few belongings on a fire escape near the Strand and headed off for King's Cross.

He knew the area well enough. He had slept round there for several years when he first came to London and he knew where the girls hung out. (...) But there was no sign of her.

He slowly walked back to the Strand, feeling more anxious than he could explain. For several weeks, he had nothing but worry for company and then, without warning, she was there again. She just arrived one day and moved back into the doorway as if she had never been away, with her hands in the pockets of her little black jacket and a big grin on her face. She looked a little rough. She had been in and out of all kinds of danger which she barely seemed to recognise — she had been arrested for begging — but the main thing was that she was back in his doorway, where he could keep an eye on her, where she said she felt safe. It warmed his heart to see her.

From time to time now, she slipped away from him again, usually when Mick or some other young man came by and started whispering about drugs they had for her. Bob always shrugged and wished she wouldn't go, but she always came back to him, cheerful and smiling.

He began to feel he was really doing some good here, offering her one stable place in a world gone mad. He even had the courage to confront her about the drugs, but as soon as he opened his mouth, he sensed he'd gone too far. "Is it worth it?" he asked her. "For God's sake, do something different. It's dangerous." She just shrugged and walked away. So he was content to be silent, to

be her refuge when she needed him. (...) Since he had taken her under his wing, he'd never seen her look frightened, as she had on that first night. He had no idea why she had run away from her home. (...) The important thing was that she had stayed with him. (...)

She seemed to be getting very 'streetwise', finding out the best pitches for begging, where to get a free cup of tea, how to pick up unsold cakes at the end of the day from the pastry shop by Waterloo Bridge. She'd always come back at night-time with a grin for Bob. And he'd just say, "You're all right then?" and they'd settle down in the doorway together. Bob liked the way she always seemed to be so merry and bright. He soon found out he was wrong.

She went off one day, in her usual way, and didn't come back at night. And weeks later, when she did finally surface, she told him immediately that she had been in hospital because she had taken an overdose. She told him she had wanted to die. Bob struggled to make sense of it. It seemed she'd fallen in and out with Mick once too often, she had been messing about with drugs again, and Bob was pretty sure she'd been selling herself. Suddenly she just didn't seem to know where to go or how to get there. But Bob wasn't about to give up.

She had been one step away from disaster and he was determined to help her if he could. He encouraged her to stay with him during the day, selling the Big Issue, and at night he sheltered her. He kept on gently working away at her, shaking his weather-beaten head sadly at her over her fiddling with drugs and feeling that he might finally be getting somewhere. A couple of weeks later when some bloke came along at two in the morning and started whispering to her, he wasn't too worried. She said: "Bob, I've got to go off for an hour. All right? See you later."

He didn't like it, but he was sure she would be back. When morning came and there was still no sign of her, he was puzzled. He tried not to worry — this was just the way that young people were — and he waited for her to turn up again the next time she needed a rest. He didn't hear anything for several days until her boyfriend Mick walked by one afternoon.

"You hear what's happened to Sharon?" he said.

Bob shook his head and said he had no idea. "She's dead", said Mick. "They found her in a gents' toilet in New Cross."

Bob Easton sat alone in his doorway. All along the Strand, the shoppers and the tourists came and went, (...) taxis lining up outside the Savoy. All these people. He didn't know any of them.

He walked heavily to a phone-box and called the police but he couldn't find anyone who knew what had happened. He kept asking on the street if anyone knew about the funeral — if anyone knew what had happened to Sharon. Someone said she had been pregnant — maybe it was from one of her punters. Bob didn't know. He felt powerless. More than that, he felt sad.

All the time he had been helping her and trying to protect her, he had felt as though he was doing her a favour. Now that she was gone, he realised that she had been helping him, too, even though neither of them had seen it at the time. He had been a father-figure to her, but she had become like the family he had never had. It sounded soft but the truth was that she had become his friend and he had come to like her very much. (...)

Bob Easton couldn't make any sense of what had happened. Sharon had left the safety of his doorway and drifted into a world he barely understood. Most of the old homeless were on the street because they were misfits of one kind or another. Some of them were proud to be misfits, happy to be out there on their own. And Sharon had been a little like that herself, taking refuge in the streets.

But most of the young ones were different. They weren't escaping onto the streets. There was no escape for them because the source of their pain was the whole of their lives — useless, pointless, hopeless lives. They had grown up to believe there was nothing for them in life — no real interest, no good work, no genuine help, no future worth fighting for. (...)

Bob Easton sits alone now, shaking his old head. He often thinks about her, and he wants people to know what happened. He doesn't know whether she wanted to die or whether it was simply an inevitable accident. Either way, the truth remains that one doorway was not enough of a world for her. (...)

Selfstudy

Present simple / Present perfect
Adjectives / Adverbs

G p. 83 + 84

1 Present simple or present perfect

Read about Ann who is an art student. Fill the blank spaces with the verbs listed, putting them in either the present simple or the present perfect.

be, feel, keep, leave, live, make, try, visit, work

Like many other students, I (1) .... to

maintain a workable lifestyle. I (2) ....
on an allowance from my parents so far, but I

(3, *occasionally*) .... as a

city guide which (4) .... me some
money for 'luxuries', such as clothes and socialising.

Since I started university I (5, *always*) ....

.... the need to participate in non-academic activities, too. During the past two years

I (6) .... on holiday twice and

I (7) .... both Paris and Amsterdam.

I (8, *always*) .... lots of
friends while travelling. We (9, *regularly*)

.... in touch by E-mail.

2 -ing or -ed

Fill the blank spaces with the following adjectives, using the ending *-ing* if necessary, for example:
*The book was interest**ing**. I got so interest**ed** and read it in one day.*

bored, disappointed, excited, satisfied, shocked, surprised, tired, worried

1 The applicant hoped to get the job and felt very

.... when he finally didn't.

2 Almost everybody closed their eyes at the

.... sight of the accident.

3 Her voice sounded rather ....,
she almost started crying.

4 The party was really ...., there
was even a band playing live music.

5 She knew very little about him and was most

.... to hear that he was a millionaire.

6 It was the most .... trip, they
travelled for nine hours altogether.

7 It was quite .... to listen to the
artist who explained every detail of the picture.

8 Glen passed the exam best of all and felt very

.... when he heard the results.

3 Look, feel, smell, taste, sound

Finish these sentences, using one of the verbs above and adding one of these adjectives:

burnt, cold, delicious, quite young, so sweet, terrible, tired, worried.

1 Mary has forgotten to switch off the oven on

time. The cake ....

2 Peter didn't sleep very much last night. Everybody

can see that because he ....

3 Paul noticed that his friend had a problem

because his voice ....

4 Sarah can't stand winter because she always

....

5 She loves roses in particular because they

....

6 Although Mrs Mervin is seventy she wears a mini.

People think she still ....

7 Older people usually can't stand disco music

because to them it ....

8 Most people generally love Italian food because

it ....

4 Prefixes

a) Fill the blank spaces with the opposite of the words listed, using the prefix *dis-*, *un-*, *im-* or *in-*.
believable, connected, correct, honest, obedient, organised, patient, pleasant, polite, satisfied

1 Because of the bad weather conditions, the

   flight was very ....

2 John's life is terribly ....
   that´s why he never seems to find a proper job.

3 It's absolutely .... how well
   the actor played his part.

4 While talking to her boss on the phone, the line

   was suddenly ....

5 The hotel was nice but the guests were

   .... with the food.

6 You can tell her nationality due to her

   .... pronunciation.

7 You can't trust people who are

   .... and never tell the truth.

8 The little girl was sent to bed early for being

   .... the whole day.

9 It's rather .... not to greet
   your neighbours.

10 People tend to become ....
   if they don't make progress in English fast.

b) Now write the nouns of all the words listed above.

5 Adverbs of time, frequency and manner

Read the text and add any of the adverbs listed wherever you find it appropriate.
approximately, definitely, gradually, mostly, occasionally, terribly

As soon as kids are (1) .... six

and (2) .... go to McDonald's to

buy Happy Meals, they (3) ....
understand how to deal with money. But they should

(4) .... get a kind of financial

education at school in order to (5) ....
learn to manage money on their own.

It shouldn't be (6) .... difficult
to teach children who have credit cards and multiple
bank accounts.

6 Creative writing

Choose one of these openings and write a composition of about 120 to 150 words.
1 My mood has so much to do with ...
2 I particularly remember one happy moment when ...
3 I greatly admire people who think positively and keep other people's spirits high, like ...
4 The most rewarding thing I have ever invested in was ...

Checkpoint

Write your answers on a separate piece of paper if necessary.

1 Find other time expressions for the one in bold print: I have saved a lot **so far**.

2 Add *rarely* to each sentence:
   1 I watch TV.
   2 I've met him since then.
   3 She went swimming last year.

3 Grade these adverbs of frequency:
   ☐ always   ☐ frequently   ☐ never
   ☐ occasionally ☐ rarely   ☐ regularly
   ☐ sometimes   ☐ usually

4 Translate: John worked hard when he was young but he hardly earned anything.

5 Translate: She is very well. She is very good.

6 Make a list of prefixes used to form the opposite of adjectives: un-, ...

7 Add one of these adverbs to each sentence:
   absolutely, awfully, completely, terribly.
   1 I'm exhausted.   3 I'm anxious.
   2 I'm sorry.   4 I'm sure.

8 Form the comparison and superlative of these adjectives, for example: *nice/nicer/nicest*.
   angry, bad, boring, disappointed, friendly, good, lonely, pleased, sad

9 Use the comparison and superlative form and complete the two sentences with each of these adverbs: *beautifully, well, badly*.
   She sings ... than the others. She sings ... of all.

10 Write the opposite of: I work **a lot**. He studies **more** than I do. She is **the most** intelligent of all.

11 Complete these sentences to form the comparison:
   His English is more fluent ... mine.
   He speaks ... well ... a native speaker.
   He's ... best in the class.

12 Write the questions to these answers:
   He looks like a schoolboy.   It tastes very sweet.
   Her voice sounds worried.   It smells terrible.
   The material feels very soft.

**Present perfect / Past perfect
-ing-form / Infinitive**

G p. 83 + 84

1 Remember / stop / regret / hate doing / to do s.th.

Put the verbs in brackets in either the infinitive or the -ing-form.

1 I've never really stopped (*worry*) ....

2 I clearly remember (*give*) .... you the keys.

3 I hate (*disturb*) .... you but I have an important message.

4 I regret (*not have had*) .... more time yesterday.

5 I don't regret (*tell*) .... you all about it.

6 Please remember (*type*) .... the letter.

7 She stopped (*work*) .... to say hello.

8 Did you remember (*talk*) .... to him as I requested?

2 Phrasal verbs that take the preposition 'off'

Write the correct verb and the preposition *off* in the empty spaces.

cut, go (2x), put (2), run, switch, send, set, show, take (3x), .

1 People who try to ....
by wearing exceptionally shocking clothes really

.... me ....

2 We had had to .... early

because the plane .... at 7am.

Fortunately the alarm clock ....
on time.

3 Due to her financial situation she has had to

.... the holiday trip ....

4 The robber .... with all the money and hasn't been seen since.

5 Sue appreciated .... a year ....
particularly as she loves travelling.

6 He was in the middle of an interesting conversa-

tion when the line was ....

7 The children's programme was so nice. Why have

they .... it ....?

8 People panicked the moment the light was

....

9 Peter was looking forward to finally

.... to Australia on his own.

10 There was no point in .... the letters

.... early, because it was a Sunday.

3 Present perfect or past perfect

Complete these sentences in such a way that they mean the same as the ones given. Write them on a separate piece of paper.

1 When the singing conductor returned after his holidays, the old ladies felt happy again.
It was not until ...

2 Mr Lewis was appointed chief executive two years ago. After that, the firm's profits increased.
From the moment Mr Lewis ...

3 First he worked in the sales department and then he changed to marketing.
It was only after he ...

4 He invested all his money in shares and his fortune is worth double now.
Ever since he ...

5 Jane devoted all her time to her family and then the children moved out.
After Jane ...

6 The last time she was on holiday on her own was ten years ago.
She ...

7 She is looking for a challenging job but she is still without one.
So far she ...

8 Kim took a year off before she went to university.
Soon after Kim ...

9 She finished her degree and went to America.
As soon as she ...

10 Ron doesn't know whether to study in England or in the States.
Ron (*not yet / decide*) ...

4 -ing-form or infinitive

Fill the gaps in the text below with these verbs:
care, disappear, find, gain, get, graduate, put, take,
take part, teach, travel, work.

Thousands of teenagers choose (1) ....

off going to college for a year in the hope of

(2) .... a mixture of adventure and

experience. The 'gap' year is becoming increasingly

popular both before university and after

(3) .... Often they spend their

time (4) .... abroad. Although

parents occasionally disapprove of their children

(5) .... to Singapore, Bangkok, India

and Nepal, the young generation feels the need

(6) .... their independence. They

sometimes prefer (7) .... in

voluntary jobs like (8) .... for the

sick, the handicapped and the aged people. Or they

decide (9) .... English or

(10) .... in outdoor projects. In most

cases it is perfectly acceptable (11) ....

a year off as it can often improve the chances of

eventually (12) .... a job later.

5 Creative writing

Read the advertisement below which was published under the heading ***Advertise your skills***. Write one yourself in complete sentences. Choose any type of job you'd like to do and use phrases like:
I suppose I would …
I could imagine myself …
I'm particularly interested in …
I'm very skilled / talented / good at …
I think I could manage to …

> British Graphic designer, 35, seeks work in Italy.
> Fully qualified and experienced. Self-motivated, enthusiastic, can work under pressure. Studied computer graphics. Learning Italian at present. Any work in Italy considered which allows me to use my skills.
> Contact B. Wilkinson, Fax: UK (44) 273 68 4507

Checkpoint

Write your answers on a separate piece of paper if necessary.

1 How do you ask questions in the past simple? Were you …? Could you …? and …?
2 Write the past tense forms of these verbs: be, do, fall, feel, learn, make, prefer, sit, study.
3 Add *last year* (1) or *so far* (2) to the right sentence: I worked hard ☐. I've worked hard ☐.
4 Match the sentences with these words:
   a) now,   b) then,   c) up to now,   d) before that.
   1 ☐ She used to live in Paris.
   2 ☐ She had always wanted to live abroad.
   3 ☐ She has had to learn three languages.
   4 ☐ She keeps in touch with her friends by e-mail.
5 Match the beginnings with the endings:
   1 I have been there. ☐ a) long before you came.
   2 I was there. ☐ b) that's why I'm late.
   3 I had been there. ☐ c) some time ago.
6 Rewrite the sentences as one sentence, using the word(s) in brackets.
   1 She lived in Paris. Then she settled in London. (*before*)
   2 She moved to Australia. She bought a house there. (*soon after*)
7 Translate: I've had my car **for** two years. I had a car **for** two years.
8 Translate: I've known him **since** 1970. **Since** she is disabled she can't go to school.
9 Match the definitions with these sentences:
   1 ☐ He used to hate school.
   2 ☐ He is used to travelling.
   3 ☐ He used his laptop for meetings.
   4 ☐ The car used a lot of petrol.
   a) be accustomed to,   b) consume,
   c) employ s.th. for a purpose,
   d) expressing a frequent action in the past
10 Write the questions to the sentences above.

Selfstudy
Progressive and simple tense forms
-ing-form / Infinitive

G p. 86 + 88

1 Prepositions, infinitive or -ing-form

Fill the boxes with one of the prepositions listed and write the verbs in brackets on the lines. Use either the infinitive or the *-ing*-form.

about, for, in, of, on (2x), to (3x), with

According (1) [   ] psychologists, the behaviour of women, (2) [   ] which the fashion industry depends, is actually a product of their desire

(3, *appear*) .... avant-garde. (4, *wear*) .... new colours is a

way (5, *demonstrate*) [   ] ....
that you are innovative. The fashion business is

(6, *change*) [   ] .... colour, length and cut each season. Women should never get

bored (7, *wear*) [   ] .... the same style for a long time. For a woman it is very

important (8, *dress*) ....
well. Of course, a number of them usually look

(9) [   ] a dress that they feel comfortable

(10) [   ] and that they know they will carry

(11, *wear*) [   ] .... for more than one season. They therefore don't mind

(12, *spend*) .... a lot of

money on it.

2 Progressive or simple form

Put the verbs in brackets into the right tense. Use the progressive form if necessary.

1 By the time he arrived, she (*wait*) ....
.... for more than an hour.

2 As technology develops, the job market
(*seem to get*) ....
more and more interesting.

3 The lorry driver looked extremely tired.
He (*must / drive*) ....
for hours!

4 Look, I (*be*) ....
shopping. I (*spend*) ....
more than 100 pounds.

5 The passengers (*check in*) ....
.... when suddenly the alarm went off.

6 Police (*still / search*) ....
for the missing child.

7 Would you like to visit me tomorrow at eight?
I (*give*) .... a party
for all my friends.

8 I (*think*) .... about
moving to Australia for quite some time, but I
can't decide.

9 When I last saw her she (*still / live*) ....
.... with her parents.

10 Jane (*might / eat*) ....
too much, because she didn't feel well last night.

11 Next year we (*live*) ....
in our house for ten years.

12 People (*constantly / complain*) ....
.... about the pollution, but
so far they (*change*) ....
their habits.

3 Progressive or simple form

Fill the blank spaces with the following verbs, using the progressive or the simple form of the past and past perfect.

announce, be, come, begin, expand, feel, move, wear, write

As the first autumn and winter collections

(1) .... to arrive in boutiques and

department stores last year, fashion editors

(2, *already*) ....

about the delights of the new 'in' colour. Black

(3) .... the choice of many women

since the early 1990s. And now, almost overnight,

brown (4) .... into vogue.

Everybody (5) .... brown. But by

the time a number of women (6) ....

courageous enough to wear brown and

(7) .... their wardrobes, the

fashion world (8, *already*) ....

.... its next colour. Grey was the new brown.

Fashion (9, *simply*) .... on.

4 Creative writing

Read this advert which really appeared in a newspaper. What would you answer this person? Write a short letter. In case you are interested in the authentic answer, turn to the key on page 73.

Help!

I am desperate. I have no symptoms of any kind; I take no pills or any other medicine. I sleep like a baby. I have never felt the need to follow any regimen of diet or exercise. I am disgustingly healthy. So I have nothing to contribute to general conversation and I feel a social outcast. At the age of 72, something must be seriously wrong. What should I do?   JAC, Hamstead

Checkpoint

Write your answer on a separate piece of paper if necessary.

1 Translate: He seems to be working hard.
   He seemed to be working hard.
   He seemed to have been working hard.
2 Translate: The child appears to be dreaming.
   He appeared so kind.
3 Write similar sentences like the example given, using the words listed: 'I didn't **want** him to **go**.
   1 expect / come, 2 mean / do it, 3 request / help, 4 advise / marry her, 5 encourage / leave.
4 Write the questions to the sentences above, for example: *Did you want him to go?*
5 Match the sentences with their meaning.
   1 ☐ She's always talking about her health.
   2 ☐ She always talks about her dog.
   3 ☐ She constantly watches her weight.
   4 ☐ She's constantly watching me.
   a) Regularly.   b) She's getting onto my nerves.
6 Add a preposition and put the verbs into the right form.

   1 I'm looking forward .... (*see*) .... you.
   2 Do you object .... (*go*) .... by bus?
   3 I'm used .... (*work*) .... late.
   4 He prefers (*walk*) ....
      (*drive*) ....

7 Translate: I'm having tea.
   He's having great difficulties.
8 Translate: 1 I was crossing the street when I saw him. I crossed the street when I saw him.
   2 They were having dinner when he came. They had dinner when he came.
9 Correct these sentences:
   1 While I had a shower, he was phoning me.
   2 I stopped working as soon as he was coming.
   3 They were having a Fiat for ten years.
   4 Whenever she was calling, he was out.
   5 We are living here since 1990.
   6 By the time we are leaving, the sun will be shining.
10 Match the sentences:
   1 ☐ I'm having my car checked.
   2 ☐ I have checked my car.
   3 ☐ He's repairing my TV.
   4 ☐ He's just had his TV repaired.
   a) Look, it works again.
   b) I'm afraid, it's not available at the moment.
11 Translate the sentences above.
12 Translate: 1 He could be travelling by bus today as it is raining. 2 We might be going on holiday next week.

Selfstudy
Conditionals and wishes

G p. 86

1 Conditional I, II and III and wishes

Complete the following sentences.

1 Robert was waiting for the weather to improve but finally decided not to stay any longer.

If the weather ....

....

2 He only goes on holiday provided he's offered a cheap last-minute ticket.

Unless ....

....

3 Ninety-year-old Mrs Marlow never had enough money to travel by plane.

She would ....

....

4 Since my friend speaks Italian, we went to Italy instead of Spain.

If ....

....

5 I'll accept his invitation if he asks me.

Provided that ....

....

6 As long as I have no hotel confirmation, I won't book my flight.

Unless ....

....

7 John had been thinking of emigrating to Canada, but his girl friend didn't agree.

He might ....

....

8 Frank hasn't been on holiday for a long time.

It's time ....

....

9 Kate has no idea where Mike lives.

She wishes ....

....

10 As we were not well-informed about the prices, we decided not to go there.

If we ....

....

2 Conditional I, II and III and wishes

Put the verb in brackets into the right form.

1 If Sue (*have*) .... a year off when she

was young, she (*spend*) ....
it in three different countries.

2 She (*be*) .... much better at languages

now, if she (*not hesitate*) ....
then to take the chances offered.

3 Provided she (*win*) .... in the lottery,

she (*travel*) .... to Australia one day.

4 If it (*be / not*) .... for her two cats, she

(*attend*) ....
an English course in Malta last year.

5 Supposing she (*know*) .... some

French, she (*certainly / be given*) ....

.... a better pay.

6 If Sue (*really / want*) ....

to take a year off, her parents (*support*) ....

.... her financially.

7 If only she (*be*) .... more ambitious she

(*undoubtedly / achieve*) ....

.... a lot more.

8 Sue knows that unless she (*try*) ....

harder she (*never / succeed*) ....

....

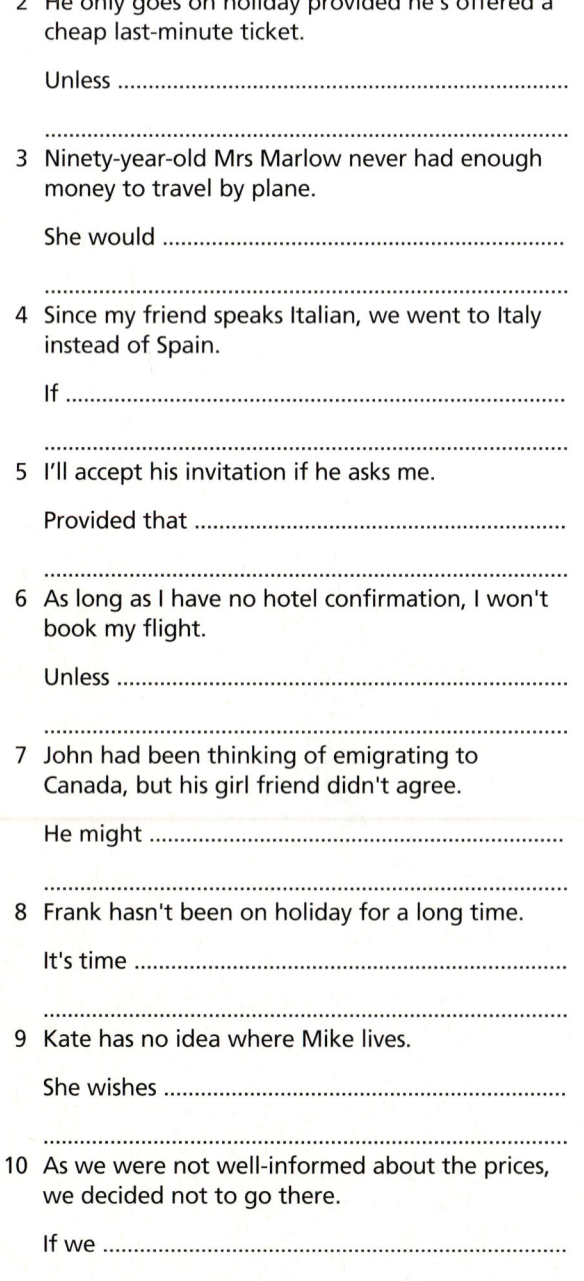

3 Common mistakes using conditionals

Rewrite all the sentences that are incorrect. Careful: three sentences are correct.

1 I'll tell you as soon as I'll hear from him.
2 He always asks her not to lock the door in case he arrives late.
3 I'll wait for you provided you'll give me a ring.
4 You would better save some money if you want to buy a car.
5 If only he wouldn't have asked me.
6 If he'd have asked me, I would have refused.
7 I'd go now if I'd be you.
8 When I have more time, I'll learn Spanish.
9 I might have agreed if he would have asked.
10 Just call me if you are ready.
11 I would buy it, provided I had enough money.
12 If John had the opportunity, he would have taken a year off.

4 Creative writing

You have discovered the advertisement below in a travel agency. The job offered seems attractive to you. Write a fax to the organisation expressing your interest. Make certain concessions and include some of these phrases: On condition that ..., provided that ..., unless ..., as long as ..., if ..., in case ....

Checkpoint

Write your answer on a separate piece of paper if necessary.

1 Change each of these sentences into the other two types of conditionals:
   1 If you'd spoken clearly, we'd have understood.
   2 We'll call you if he doesn't come.
   3 I'd feel happier if you didn't smoke.

2 What's the meaning of *when* and *if* in these sentences? Match them with:
   a) not sure,
   b) sometime in the future.
   1 ☐ I'll tell him if I see him.
   2 ☐ I'll tell him when I see him.
   3 ☐ He'll call you when he's in town.
   4 ☐ She promised to visit him if she goes out.
   5 ☐ I'll buy the book when I go shopping.

3 Rewrite this sentence without changing its meaning:
   If you didn't want me to, I wouldn't do it.
   a) Provided ... . b) Unless ... . c) Supposing ...

4 Use *unless* instead of *if*:
   1 If it doesn't rain, I'll come round.
   2 If the price is reasonable, I'll book the hotel.
   3 If he doesn't turn up on time, I'll leave.
   4 If there are less than 20 people, the tour won't take place.

5 Translate:
   1 It's about time the train arrived.
   2 It's high time you paid the bills.

6 Match the sentences with the appropriate time reference: a) now, b) then.
   1 ☐ I wish I knew him.
   2 ☐ I would have done it.
   3 ☐ She had better do it.
   4 ☐ What if he had gone?
   5 ☐ He'd hate to do it.
   6 ☐ I wish I'd done more.
   7 ☐ If only he'd seen me.
   8 ☐ It's time we got married.
   9 ☐ If only he'd say yes.
   10 ☐ We would have had to read it twice to understand the meaning.

7 What does *'d* mean in each sentence? Match the sentences with either: a) would or b) had.
   1 ☐ She'd need to study more.
   2 ☐ We'd had to hurry before we got there.
   3 ☐ He'd have to sell his car.
   4 ☐ They'd do it.
   5 ☐ You'd better leave.
   6 ☐ What she'd said was new to me.
   7 ☐ They'd go there, but they can't.
   8 ☐ If only we'd had more time.
   9 ☐ You'd have to ask him.
   10 ☐ I'd rather you didn't go.

5 Selfstudy
The passive
Reported speech

G p. 87

1 Present and future passive
Fill the gaps, considering the right tense.

In the future, your house (1, *control*) ....
.... by intelligent instruments that
register a variety of information. The results

(2, *then / pass*) .... across
the network to a personal computer (PC). People in a

room (3, *detect*) .... by
infrared sensors and the lights (4, *switch on*) ....
.... automatically when a door

(5, *open*) .... When the
phone rings, the sound of your hi-fi (6, *automatically /*

reduce) ....
so that the call (7, *not / interrupt*) ....
.... The instructions (8, *carry out*)

.... by a central control
on your PC. Or, with the press of a button on a
digital watch, the central heating (9, *turn down*)

.... if it is too hot. Your

home (10, *turn into*) ....
a showcase for today's automation technology.

2 Active or passive forms in the past
Fill the blank spaces with the verbs in brackets. Use
the past simple, the past perfect and one infinitive.

Au pair refused entry because he was not a girl

A Swedish au pair (1, *refuse*) ....
entry into Britain because he was a man. Johan

Engeström, 19, who (2, *arrive*) ....
at Heathrow airport, (3, *question*) ....
.... for three hours by immigration officials.

He (4, *tell*) .... that au pairs

(5, *have to*) .... conform to the

rules. Immigration rules (6, *say*) ....
that an au pair should be an unmarried girl aged

17 to 27 who (7, *allow*) .... into
Britain to learn the English language.

Mr Engeström (8, *invite*) ....
by letter to the home of Sue and John Newton in

Leicester, who (9, *put*) .... an
advertisement in a newspaper in Stockholm. He

(10, *chose*) .... because Mrs Newton

didn't want her children (11, *look after*) ....
.... by a woman. (PS. The rule

(12, *change*) .... shortly after Mr

Engeström (13, *accept*) ....)

3 Have / had been (done), have / had been (doing), have / had s.th. (done)
Complete each sentence, using the right form and
tense and adding any words necessary. Write the
sentences on a separate piece of paper.
1 I'm not very enthusiastic about cleaning my car, so
I (*always / clean / my neighbour*) ...
2 Sue is extremely tired, as she (*prepare for her
exams / since May*) ...
3 When the manager came back from his meeting,
the letters (*already / write*) ...
4 Peter suddenly lost control over his car because he
(*drive / already / eight hours*) ...

5 The television still didn't work although I (*repair / only recently*) ...

6 They still can't make up their mind although the matter (*discuss / so long*) ...

7 Ron apologised for being late but argued that he (*not / inform / the change of place*) ...

8 Everybody was worried about his absence and wondered what he (*do / all day long*) ...

9 John's hair looked disastrous but he said he (*cut / last week*) ...

10 Kim was pleased with the good mark but admitted that the essay (*correct / her father*) ...

4 Reported speech

Put this extract from an article into reported speech. Write it on a separate piece of paper. Begin with: *A space expert reported yesterday ... .*

Space scientists have seen
life on Mars

A report from Washington.

A robot and spacecraft exploration of Mars is being planned soon, together with a possible manned mission. We believe that we have found reasonable evidence of past life on Mars. We don't claim that we have definite proof. But we assure you that the US space programme will put its full technological skills behind Mars exploration. We are convinced that if this discovery is confirmed, it will surely be one of the most attractive insights into our universe that science has ever uncovered.

5 Creative writing
Imagine you were the author of this article. Read and add a second paragraph to it.

Off to the future with one mouse click

Many parents are excluded from the high-technology world their children inhabit. Over the past few years "surfing the Net" has become one of the most popular teenage pastimes. In Britain, according to a recent poll on people's wish lists, buying a home computer is second only to a family holiday. Even more astonishing is a statistic from the United States which suggests that children now spend more time 'interacting' on their home personal computers than watching television. And what has already happened in America is fast catching on here.

Checkpoint

Write your answer on a separate piece of paper if necessary.

1 Write as many passive forms of this sentence as possible: It is changed.

2 Translate: The newspaper said Nicola had been found.

3 Put these sentences into reported speech:
1 "She really loves me." He told me ... .
2 "Joanna once loved me dearly." He said that ... .
3 "I don't think I'm going to win." He doubted that ... .
4 "I'm sure that police will soon have found her." She was convinced that ... .
5 "It's rather cold here." She claimed that ... .
6 "I remember seeing you." She remembered ... .
7 "It's a lovely day today!" She thought ... .
8 "Yes, we saw him last night. They admitted ... .
9 "I'll definitely visit you tomorrow morning." He promised ....

4 Put these requests into reported speech, begin with an appropriate verb:
1 "Would you be kind enough to close the door?" He kindly ...
2 "Turn the heating on, please." He ...
3 "Switch the TV off immediately!" He ...
4 "Don't forget to buy some milk." He ...

5 Put the sentences above into the passive:
1 I was kindly ...

6 Match each sentence according to whether it is a) a request or b) a normal question.
1 ☐ She always asks me to help her.
2 ☐ He asked whether I needed him.
3 ☐ They asked us to accompany them.

 p. 74

Selfstudy

Aspects of the future (will)
Infinitive constructions after passive verbs
Phrase openings / Conjunctions

G p. 85 + 87

1 Will (do) / will be (doing) / will be (done)

Fill the blank spaces with the correct tense form of the verbs in brackets.

Police pack digital brain in helmets

Police on duty in the 21st century (1, *wear*)

.... 'digital helmets' that

(2, *receive*) ....

information from computers and (3, *send*)

.... live video images
back to the station. The 1.5 billion pound project

(4, *use*) .... video and
data links to develop equipment that

(5, *provide*) ....
more information for police and other emergency
services. This project is likely to lead to technology

that (6, *enable*) ....

the next generation of police to send live video
pictures of street scenes back to headquarters.

Helmets (7, *fit*) .... with

new headsets that (8, *include*) ....

.... a camera and an antenna to

transmit digital video.

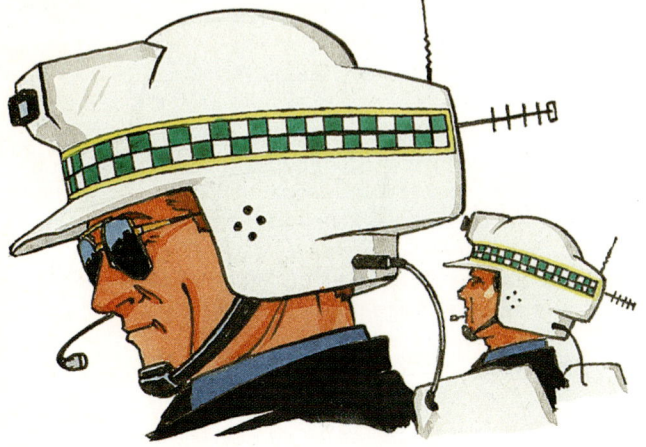

2 Will have (done) / will have been (done)

Finish each of the following sentences without
changing the meaning of the sentence before. Write
the sentences on a separate piece of paper.
An American company is developing a permanent
watch to be inserted under the skin.

1 They plan to continue the development until the
   end of this year.
   By the end of this year they (*finish*) ...

2 A laboratory will already present the first test
   results within the next three months.
   By the end of the next three months the first test
   results (*present*) ...

3 They intend to produce and implant a great
   number of watches in the future.
   Fairly soon a great number of watches (*produce /
   implant*) ...

4 In the end, people might change their critical
   minds and react positively.
   Once the watches are available, people (*probably /
   change*) ...

5 In about 2100, people will certainly not remember
   the old-fashioned type of watch.
   In a hundred years time people (*forget*) ...

3 Infinitive constructions after passive verbs

Fill the blanks with the best possible passive verb,
considering the right tense.
be believed to, be considered to, be expected to,
be known to, be supposed to, be thought to

1 Children in industrialised countries (*not*) ....

   .... work at a young age.

2 Grandparents (*commonly*) ....

   .... spoil their grand-children.

3 Holiday jobs (*still*) ....
   be part of an effective education.

4 Project work at school ....
   keep youngsters away from TV and boredom.

5 In the past, children living in rural areas (*generally*)

   ....
   help their families.

6 In the western world, child labour ....

   .... be unhealthy for a long time.

4 Phrase openings and conjunctions

Fill each blank space with at least two of the phrase openings or conjunctions listed. Some of them can be used more than once.
Careful: There's only one possibility in sentence 7.
according to, although, as, as a consequence (of), as a result (of), as soon as, because, contrary to, despite, due to, even though, for, however, in regard to, in spite of, nevertheless, on account of, shortly after, since, therefore

(1) .... it was dark, Ann went out.

She heard a cry and (2) .... phoned the police immediately. The neighbours didn't react,

(3) .... they hadn't heard anything.

(4) ...., the police believed every

detail of Ann's description (5) ....

she looked so terrified. (6) .... the morning paper had appeared, all the neighbours

were informed. (7) .... the results of the investigations, a woman had been killed the

previous night. But, (8) .... the

report, Ann is still under shock, (9) ....

.... the sudden sight of the dead body.

(10) .... the truthful reports of the press, neighbours are still sceptical about the incident.

5 Creative writing

Read the article below and write a 'Letter to the Editor', expressing your opinion about this new development. Use these phrases when adding information:

another advantage/disadvantage is, apart from that, as well as, besides, furthermore, in addition, in short, on the whole, to sum up, what is more, to conclude

Watch is implanted in skin

An American company is developing liquid crystal displays that can be inserted under the skin to create a permanent watch. A chip and battery will be fitted with a tiny screen and inserted just under the skin. The company hopes it may also be able to display blood pressure and body temperature. The battery will be recharged by holding the implant next to a charger.

Checkpoint

Write your answer on a separate piece of paper if necessary.
1 Match each sentence with its meaning:
   a) expressing an offer,
   b) expressing a future intention.
   1 ☐ I'll be gone soon.
   2 ☐ I'll give you a hand.
   3 ☐ I'll answer the phone.
   4 ☐ I'll stop smoking.
   5 ☐ I'll be ready in a minute.
   6 ☐ I'll pay for it.
2 Match the two parts of each sentence:
   1 I'll be having tea ...
   2 She will have been living here ...
   3 He will have finished his studies ...
   4 They'll call us ...
   5 I won't buy it ...
   6 He won't be having a meeting ...
   a) ☐ by early summer.
   b) ☐ unless you want me to.
   c) ☐ when you come.
   d) ☐ tomorrow morning.
   e) ☐ as soon as the plane arrives.
   f) ☐ for twenty years next month.
3 Translate: She's supposed to finish her letter.
   She's not supposed to leave early.
4 Rewrite each of the two sentences, using several conjunctions from the list below to substitute the one in bold print:
   1 She has never had a lot, **but** she is still content.
   2 **Since** he didn't catch the early train, he arrived late.
   although, as, as a consequence, as a result, because, despite the fact that, even though, nevertheless, that's why, therefore

p. 74

Selfstudy: Key

Topic 1
Selfstudy (p. 60)

1 1 try, 2 have lived, 3 occasionally work, 4 leaves, 5 have always felt, 6 have been, 7 have visited, 8 have always made, 9 regularly keep

2 1 disappointed, 2 shocking, 3 worried, 4 exciting, 5 surprised, 6 tiring, 7 boring, 8 satisfied

3 1 smells burnt. 2 looks tired. 3 sounded worried. 4 feels cold. 5 smell so sweet. 6 looks quite young. 7 sounds terrible. 8 tastes delicious.

4 a) 1 unpleasant, 2 disorganised, 3 unbelievable, 4 disconnected, 5 dissatisfied, 6 incorrect, 7 dishonest, 8 disobedient, 9 impolite, 10 impatient
b) belief, connection, correction, honesty, obedience, organisation, patience, pleasure, politeness, satisfaction

5 1 approximately, 2 occasionally, 3 mostly, 4 definitely, 5 gradually, 6 terribly

Checkpoint (p. 61)
1 up to now, until now, in my life, since then, for the last six months, during the past years
2 1 I rarely watch TV. 2 I've rarely met him since then. 3 She rarely went swimming last year.
3 always, regularly, usually, frequently, sometimes, occasionally, rarely, never
4 John arbeitete hart, als er jung war, aber er verdiente kaum etwas.
5 Es geht ihr sehr gut. Sie ist sehr gut.
6 dis- (discontent / dishonest), il- (illegal / illogical), im- (impractical / imperfect), in- (incorrect / ineffective), ir- (irresponsible / irregular), mis- (misused / misbehaved)
7 1 I'm completely (or: absolutely) exhausted. 2 I'm awfully (or: terribly) sorry. 3 I'm terribly anxious. 4 I'm absolutely (or: completely) sure.
8 angry / angrier / angriest or more / most angry, bad / worse / worst, boring / more boring / most boring, disappointed / more disappointed / most disappointed, friendly / friendlier / friendliest, good / better / best, lonely / lonelier / loneliest, pleased / more pleased / most pleased, sad / sadder / saddest
9 She sings more beautifully / better / worse than the others. She sings most beautifully / best / worst of all.
10 I work little. He studies less than I do. She is the least intelligent of all.
11 (more fluent) than, as (well) as, the (best)
12 What does he look like? What does it taste like? What does her voice sound like? What does it smell like? What does the material feel like?

Topic 2
Selfstudy (p. 62)

1 1 worrying, 2 giving, 3 to disturb, 4 not having had, 5 telling, 6 to type, 7 working, 8 to talk

2 1 show off / put me off, 2 set off / took off / went off, 3 put (the holiday trip) off, 4 ran off, 5 taking (a year) off, 6 cut off, 7 taken (it) off, 8 switched off, 9 going off, 10 sending (the letters) off

3 1 It was not until the singing conductor had returned from his holidays that the old ladies felt happy again. 2 From the moment Mr Lewis was appointed chief executive two years ago, the firm's profits have increased. 3 It was only after he had worked in the sales department that he changed to marketing. 4 Ever since he invested all his money in shares, his fortune has doubled. 5 After Jane had devoted all her time to her family, the children moved out. 6 She hasn't been on holiday on her own for the last ten years. 7 So far she hasn't found a challenging job. 8 Soon after Kim had taken a year off, she went to university. 9 As soon as she had finished her degree, she went to America. 10 Ron hasn't decided yet whether to study in England or in the States.

4 1 to put, 2 finding, 3 graduating, 4 travelling , 5 disappearing, 6 to gain, 7 working, 8 caring, 9 to teach, 10 to take part, 11 to take, 12 getting

Checkpoint (p. 63)
1 Did you ...?
2 was/were, did, fell, felt, learnt, made, preferred, sat, studied
3 I worked hard last year. I've worked hard so far.
4 1b, 2d, 3c, 4a
5 1b, 2c, 3a
6 1 Before she settled in London, she had lived in Paris. 2 Soon after she had moved to Australia, she bought a house there.
7 Ich habe mein Auto (schon/bereits) seit zwei Jahren. Ich hatte zwei Jahre lang ein Auto.
8 Ich kenne ihn (schon/bereits) seit 1970. Da sie behindert ist, kann sie nicht zur Schule gehen.
9 1d, 2a, 3c, 4b
10 1 Did he use to hate school? 2 Is he used to travelling? 3 Did he use his laptop for meetings? 4 Did the car use a lot of petrol?

Topic 3
Selfstudy (p. 64)

1 1 to, 2 on, 3 to appear, 4 Wearing, 5 of demonstrating, 6 about changing, 7 with wearing, 8 to dress, 9 for, 10 in, 11 on wearing, 12 spending

2 1 had been waiting, 2 seems to be getting,
3 must have been driving, 4 have been / have spent,
5 were checking in, 6 are still searching,
7 will be giving (or: 'm giving), 8 have been thinking,
9 was still living, 10 might have eaten, 11 will have
lived (or: will have been living), 12 are constantly
complaining / haven't changed

3 1 were beginning, 2 had already written,
3 had been, 4 had come, 5 was wearing,
6 felt, 7 expanded, 8 was already announcing,
9 was simply moving

4 Possible answer: You have written in to show off.
There are numerous bad habits you could develop to
damage your health and give you something to
contribute to general conversation among your
friends. Why not knock back a bottle of cream sherry
tonight and spend tomorrow moaning about your
hangover?

Checkpoint (p. 65)
1 Er scheint zur Zeit hart zu arbeiten. Es schien, als
ob er hart arbeitete. Es schien, als hätte er hart
gearbeitet.
2 Das Kind scheint zu träumen. Er machte einen so
netten Eindruck. / Er schien so nett.
3 1 I didn't expect him to come. 2 I didn't mean him
to do it. 3 I didn't request him to help. 4 I didn't advise
him to marry her. 5 I didn't encourage him to leave.
4 1 Did you expect him to come? 2 Did you mean
him to do it? 3 Did you request him to help? 4 Did
you advise him to marry her? 5 Did you encourage
him to leave?
5 1b, 2a, 3a, 4b
6 1 looking forward to seeing you. 2 object to going
by bus. 3 used to working late. 4 prefers walking to
driving.
7 Ich trinke gerade Tee. Er hat im Augenblick
große Schwierigkeiten.
8 1 Ich überquerte gerade die Straße, als ich ihn sah.
Ich überquerte die Straße, als ich ihn sah. / nachdem
ich ihn gesehen hatte. 2 Sie waren gerade beim
Abendessen, als er kam. Nachdem er gekommen
war / Als er kam, aßen sie zu Abend.
9 1 While I was having a shower, he phoned me.
2 I stopped working as soon as he came.
3 They had a Fiat for ten years. 4 Whenever she called,
he was out. 5 We have been living here since 1990.
6 By the time we leave, the sun will be shining.
10 1b, 2a, 3b, 4a
11 1 Ich lasse gerade mein Auto überprüfen.
2 Ich habe (soeben) mein Auto überprüft.
3 Er repariert gerade meinen Fernseher.
4 Er hat seinen Fernseher (soeben) reparieren lassen.
12 Möglicherweise fährt er heute mit dem Bus, da
es regnet. / Es kann sein, dass er heute mit dem Bus
fährt, da es regnet. 2 Es kann sein, dass wir nächste
Woche in Urlaub fahren. / Vielleicht fahren wir
nächste Woche in Urlaub.

Topic 4
Selfstudy (p. 66)
1 1 If the weather had improved, Robert would
have stayed longer.
 2 Unless he is offered a cheap last-minute ticket,
he doesn't (or: won't) go on holiday.
 3 She would have travelled by plane if she had had
enough money.
 4 If my friend spoke Spanish, we'd have gone to
Spain rather than to Italy.
 5 Provided that he asks me, I'll accept his invitation.
 6 Unless I have a hotel confirmation, I won't book
my flight.
 7 He might have emigrated to Canada if his
girlfriend had agreed.
 8 It's time Frank went on holiday.
 9 She wishes she knew where Mike lived.
10 If we had been better informed about the prices,
we would have gone there.

2 1 had had / would have spent, 2 would be / had
not hesitated, 3 wins / will travel, 4 weren't
(or: hadn't been) / would have attended, 5 knew /
would certainly be given, 6 had really wanted /
would have supported, 7 she were (or: was) / she
would undoubtedly achieve (or: have achieved),
8 tries (or: tried) / will (or: would) never succeed.

3 1 as soon as I hear from him, 2 correct, 3 provided
you give me a ring, 4 You had better save, 5 he
hadn't asked me, 6 If he had asked me, 7 if I were
you, 8 correct (or: If I have more time, I'll learn
Spanish). 9 if he had asked. 10 when you are ready,
11 correct, 12 If John had had the opportunity

Checkpoint (p. 67)
1 1 If you speak clearly, we'll understand. If you
spoke clearly, we would understand. 2 We would call
you if he didn't come. We would have called you if
he hadn't come. 3 I'll feel happier if you don't smoke.
I would have felt happier if you hadn't smoked.
2 1a, 2b, 3b, 4a, 5b
3 a) Provided you wanted me to, I would do it.
b) Unless you wanted me to, I wouldn't do it.
c) Supposing you wanted me to, I would do it.
4 1 Unless it rains, I'll come round. 2 Unless the price
is reasonable, I won't book the hotel. 3 Unless he turns
up on time, I'll leave. 4 Unless there are 20 people,
the tour won't take place.
5 1 Der Zug sollte schon längst da sein. / Es ist an
der Zeit, dass der Zug kommt. 2 Es ist höchste Zeit,
dass du die Rechnungen zahlst.
6 1a, 2b, 3a, 4b, 5a, 6b, 7b, 8a, 9a, 10b
7 1a, 2b, 3a, 4a, 5b, 6b, 7a, 8b, 9a, 10a

Topic 5
Selfstudy (p. 68)

1 1 will be controlled, 2 will then be passed, 3 will be detected, 4 will be switched on, 5 is opened, 6 will automatically be reduced, 7 is not interrupted, 8 will be carried out, 9 will be turned down, 10 will be turned into

2 1 was refused, 2 arrived (or: had arrived), 3 was questioned, 4 was told, 5 had to (or: have to), 6 said (or: say), 7 was (or: is) allowed, 8 had been invited, 9 had put, 10 had been chosen, 11 to be looked after, 12 was changed, 13 had been accepted

3 1 ... I always have it cleaned by my neighbour.
2 ... she has been preparing for her exams since May.
3 ... the letters had already been written.
4 ... he had already been driving for eight hours.
5 ... I had (or: had had) it repaired only recently.
6 ... the matter has been discussed for so long.
7 ... he had not been informed about the change of place. 8 ... he had been doing all day long.
9 ... he had had it cut last week. 10 ... the essay had been corrected by her father.

4 A space expert reported yesterday that a robot and spacecraft exploration of Mars was being planned soon, together with a possible manned mission. They/Experts believed that they had found reasonable evidence of past life on Mars. They didn't claim that they had definite proof. But they assured us that the US space programme would put its full technological skills behind Mars exploration. They were convinced that if this discovery was confirmed, it would surely be one of the most attractive insights into our universe that science had ever uncovered.

Checkpoint (p. 69)

1 Present: It is being changed. Past: It was changed. It was being changed. Infinitive: It is / was to be changed. Present perfect: It has been changed. Past perfect: It had been changed. Future: It will be changed. It is going to be changed. Future perfect: It will have been changed. Modal structures: It may / might / can / could / should / would / must (has to) be / ought to be changed. It might / could / should / would / must have been changed.
2 Die Zeitung berichtete, dass Nicola gefunden worden sei. / In der Zeitung stand (geschrieben), dass ... .
3 1 ... she really loved him. 2 ... Joanna had once loved him dearly. 3 ... he was going to win.
4 ... police would soon have found her (or: the baby).
5 ... it was rather cold there. 6 ... having seen me.
7 ... it was a lovely day then. 8 ... having seen (or: that they had seen) him the previous night.

9 ... to visit him (or: her / them) the next (or: following) morning.
4 1 He kindly asked (or: requested) me to close the door. 2 He asked (or: told) me to turn the heating on. 3 He ordered (or: wanted / told) me to switch the TV off immediately. 4 He reminded me (not to forget) to buy some milk.
5 1 I was kindly asked (or: requested) to ... .
2 I was asked (or: told) to ... . 3 I was ordered to ... .
4 I was reminded to ... .
6 1a, 2b, 3a

Topic 6
Selfstudy (p. 70)

1 1 will be wearing, 2 will receive, 3 will be sending, 4 will use (or: will be using), 5 will provide, 6 will enable, 7 will be fitted, 8 will include

2 1 ... they will have finished the development.
2 ... the first test results will already have been presented.
3 ... will have been produced and implanted.
4 ... people will probably have changed their minds.
5 ... people will certainly have forgotten

3 1 are not supposed to, 2 are commonly known to, 3 are still thought (or: considered) to, 4 is believed (or: thought) to, 5 were generally expected to, 6 has been considered (or: believed) to

4 1 Although, Even though; 2 as a result, as a consequence, therefore; 3 because, as, since, for; 4 However, Nevertheless; 5 because, as, since, for; 6 Shortly after, As soon as; 7 According to; 8 contrary to, according to; 9 due to, on account of, as a consequence of, as a result of; 10 Despite, In spite of

Checkpoint (p. 71)

1 1b, 2a, 3a, 4b, 5b, 6a
2 1c, 2f, 3a, 4e (c, d), 5b, 6d (c)
3 Sie sollte ihren Brief fertig schreiben. (Es wird von ihr erwartet, dass sie ihren Brief fertig schreibt.) Sie sollte nicht früh weggehen.
4 1 She is still content, although (or: even though) she has never had a lot. She has never had a lot; nevertheless, she is still content. Despite the fact that she has never had a lot, she is still content.
2 Because (or: As) he didn't catch the early train, he arrived late. He didn't catch the early train, that's why (or: as a result / as a consequence / therefore) he arrived late.

Information gap activities Student A

Topic 1: Activity reading
Task 3 (p. 43)
Student A: Read these extracts describing some of the actions taking place in the room. Then, with two other A-partners, answer the following questions and make some notes. Once you have completed the task, turn back to page 43.

1 What kind of room is it?
2 What's the atmosphere in the room like?
3 What's the relationship between the two characters? Do they like each other?
4 In what way do the two people differ in personality?
5 Is there a problem? If so, what kind of problem is it?
6 What are their individual needs?

– The American wife stood at the window looking out.
– The husband went on reading, lying propped up with the two pillows at the foot of the bed.
– She opened the door of the room. George was on the bed, reading.
– She sat down on the bed.
– She went over and sat in front of the mirror of the dressing-table, looking at herself with the hand glass. She studied her profile, first one side and then the other. Then she studied the back of her head and her neck.
– George looked up and saw the back of her neck, clipped close like a boy's.
– George shifted his position on the bed. He hadn't looked away from her since she started to speak.
– She laid the mirror down on the dresser and went over to the window and looked out.
– George was reading again.
– She was looking out of the window.
– George was not listening. He was reading his book.

Topic 3: Unit 5
Task 7 (p. 21)
Student A: Read your words to your partner one by one and listen to his/her matching suggestions. Together form and write word pairs with your word-lists. Don't look at each other's page. Listen only!

make	help	support
solve	face	build up
give a sense of	develop	co-operate
improve	take	

Now, write a short text for an educational magazine on the value of team sports. Use as many word combinations as possible and add a headline, too.

Topic 3: Language in action
Task 4 (p. 24)
Student A: Read the story below and with another A-student work out four comprehension questions. Write them down individually. Then, find a partner from group B. Exchange your questions and try to answer your partner's questions using your imagination. Don't correct your partner's answers nor give any hints. At the end, read each other's story.

Bus Burglars
Two armed bandits had been waiting for several hours for a passing bus in the Guatemalan countryside when they finally saw one approaching in the distance. The thieves were convinced that the oncoming bus contained wealthy tourists and therefore blocked the road with their car. However, while the bandits were happily boarding the bus, one of the passengers got up and arrested them on the spot. The unlucky team found the bus to contain 40 armed policemen who were being transferred to another post. The police politely informed the bandits of their mistake and gently escorted them to the nearest prison cell.

Topic 5: Unit 10
Task 3 (p. 34)
Student A: Read your text and with another A-student answer the following questions. Make individual notes.
1 What is the child most scared of?
2 How does she react towards the daily TV news?
3 To what extent does the child like being scared?
4 When does the child feel most secure?

Olivia, aged seven:
When I was about four years old, there was this man who wanted me and he tried to kidnap me to sell me to someone. But now I'm not scared about that any more. I'm scared about these aliens I saw on TV. They had one huge black eye and a mouth in the wrong place and they made a sort of dragon come and breathe fire. I was terrified, but I like scary things. I like scary stories when I'm safe at home. I don't like it if my parents are out for long. I was scared stiff once when there was a fight in the street and I thought the crowd would set fire to our home – as I had seen on the news before. I'm sometimes very frightened when the news is on. The worst thing I could ever imagine happening is my bedroom curtain – someone pulling it down and just killing me. Just like that. Piff!

Now, form A/B/C groups and compare your answers with the help of your notes only. What do the three children have in common?

Student A Information gap activities

Topic 5: Language in action
Task 3 (p. 36)
Student A: Yesterday, you received a letter from 'International TV-Corporation'. Talk to your partner and report in detail what information the letter contained (statements 1-10). Use reported speech with these phrase openings:

The letter said that ... .
It also mentioned that ... .
Furthermore it stated that ... .
ITC promised that ... .
It also confirmed that ... .
In addition, the letter said that ... .
Last but not least, they asked me to ... .

1 You were successful in our competition last week!
2 You are the fortunate winner from 2 million participants.
3 You scored 100%!
4 You are going to spend a three-week holiday in Florida!
5 You don't need a single cent. Everything is free for you.
6 Additionally, you will be sent a $ 1000 cheque.
7 You will be flying First Class on an airline of your choice.
8 We are going to send you a list of hotels to choose from.
9 A car will be provided free of charge for the three weeks.
10 You will be accompanied by a private guide throughout your holiday.

Give us a call or send a fax. We are ready for your take-off!

Are you excited about your prize? Share your feelings with your partner and discuss these questions:
1 Will you accept the offer?
2 To what extent would this way of spending a holiday suit you?
3 What do you intend to do apart from the things offered?
4 Would you rather go on your partner's holiday?

Topic 6: Activity reading
Task 2 (p. 56)
Student A: Read this text and with another A-student answer the following questions according to what you believe the situation could be like. Take individual notes. Then find a partner from the other group. Form A/B-pairs and compare the two characters by reporting your answers.

Bob had been living on the streets of London for the best part of 11 years now and he had learned a lot about survival and, in particular, he had learned that the streets are no place for friendship. He knew a lot of people out there and he liked some of them well enough and he was perfectly happy to stop and pass the time of day with them. But basically he always reckoned he was on his own. As far as he could see, that was the only way to survive – find your own food, guard your own patch, each man for himself. It was a bloody jungle out there.

1 How old is Bob, do you think?
2 What kind of character is he?
3 How does he feel living on the street?
4 How does he relate to other people?
5 How dependent is he on other people?
6 Is he the kind of person who can survive on the street?

Student B Information gap activities

Topic 1: Activity reading
Task 3 (p. 43)
Student B: Read parts of the conversation the two Americans were having in the room. Then, with two other B-partners, answer the following questions and take some notes. Once you have completed the task, turn back to page 43.
1 What kind of room is it?
2 What's the atmosphere in the room like?
3 What's the relationship between the two characters? Do they like each other?
4 In what way do the two people differ in personality?
5 Is there a problem? If yes, what kind of problem is it?
6 What are their individual needs?

"I'm going down and get that kitty."
"I'll do it."
"No, I'll get it. The poor kitty out trying to keep dry under a table."
"Don't get wet."

"Did you get the cat?"
"It was gone."
"Wonder where it went to?"

"I wanted it so much. I don't know why I wanted it so much. I wanted that poor kitty. It isn't any fun to be a poor kitty out in the rain."

"Don't you think it would be a good idea if I let my hair grow out?"
"I like it the way it is."
"I get so tired of it. I get so tired of looking like a boy."
"You look pretty darn nice."
"I want to pull my hair back tight and smooth and make a big knot at the back that I can feel."
"I want to have a kitty to sit on my lap and purr when I stroke her."
"Yeah?"

"And I want to eat at a table with my own silver and I want candles.
And I want it to be spring and I want to brush my hair out in front of a mirror and I want a kitty and I want some new clothes."
"Oh, shut up and get something to read."

"Anyway, I want a cat. I want a cat. I want a cat now. If I can't have long hair or any fun, I can have a cat."

Topic 3: Unit 5
Task 7 (p. 21)
Student B: Listen to your partner's words and choose possible matching words from your list. Together form and write word pairs with your word-lists. Don't look at each other's page. Listen only!

security	decisions	problems
your own identity	difficulties	each other
your social life	the weaker	pride
courage and confidence	with others	

Now, write a short text for an educational magazine on the value of team sports. Use as many word combinations as possible and add a headline, too.

Topic 3: Language in action
Task 4 (p. 24)
Student B: Read this story and with another B-student work out four comprehension questions. Write them down individually. Then, find a partner from group A. Exchange your questions and try to answer your partner's questions using your imagination. Don't correct your partner's answers nor give any hints.
At the end, read each other's story.

Father of 21
'Superdad' Mr John Knight, 58, the man who fathered twenty-one children, died last Wednesday. He suddenly suffered a heart attack while he was jogging between his two homes. Mr Knight had twelve children by his wife Carole, aged 49, and nine by his girlfriend Clare, aged 53. He had never lived with his girlfriend but he regularly visited her and the children. In order to support his children, he had been receiving social security payments for almost 15 years. Two councils spent a total of £50,000 buying houses for his two families. After Mr Knight had found a new love, aged 39, he and his wife parted and their 20-year marriage finally ended in divorce. He had consequently been living on his own until his final day.

Topic 5: Unit 10
Task 3 (p. 34)
Student B: Read your text and with another B-student answer the following questions. Take individual notes.
1 What is the child most scared of?
2 How does he react towards the daily TV news?
3 To what extent does the child like being scared?
4 When does the child feel most secure?

Philip, aged nine:
I watch the telly news all the time, just because it's interesting and it doesn't make me worry about my own life. Everything on the news is upsetting, but the things are not exactly likely – are they? The Atomic bomb was just horrible, though, but it didn't make me feel it could happen here. We used to write down the news in a journal every day at school, but I'm glad we don't do that now. It's not that sort of thing which frightens me, though. I'm really scared of the bigger boys from our other local school. They steal and spit at us. The funny thing is, I like being scared by books. If you're reading them at home, with Mum and Dad in, you can really enjoy them. But sometimes in bed later, I'm frightened by the shadows on the wall.

Now, form A/B/C groups and compare your answers with the help of your notes only. What do the three children have in common?

Student B Information gap activities

Topic 5: Language in action
Task 3 (p. 36)
Student B: Yesterday, you received a letter from 'International TV-Corporation'. Talk to your partner and report in detail what information the letter contained (statements 1-10). Use reported speech with these phrase openings:

The letter said that ... .
It also mentioned that ... .
Furthermore it stated that ... .
ITC promised that ... .
It also confirmed that ... .
In addition, the letter said ... .
Last but not least, they asked me to ... .

1 This is the moment you have longed for!
2 You have won the first prize in our monthly competition!
3 Your entry has been chosen because it was the best!
4 We are offering you a fascinating three-week trip around the world.
5 Everything will be paid for!
6 You will soon be receiving a shopping cheque book to be used anywhere.
7 American Airline will safely take you to the most famous airports and places.
8 You will be staying at the most spectacular hotels.
9 A private chauffeur will pick you up at every airport and take you around.
10 Don't hesitate. Take your chance and leave at once!

Give us a call or send a fax. We are ready for your take-off!

Are you excited about your prize? Share your feelings with your partner and discuss these questions.
1 Will you accept the offer?
2 To what extent would this way of spending a holiday suit you?
3 What do you intend to do apart from the things offered?
4 Would you rather go on your partner's holiday?

Topic 6: Activity reading
Task 2 (p. 56)
Student B: Read this text and with another B-student answer the following questions according to what you believe the situation could be like. Take individual notes. Then find a partner from the other group. Form A/B-pairs and compare the two characters by reporting your answers.

Sharon looked completely lost, wandering along the Strand in the dark with a little black jacket pulled tight around her top. She was a cheerful little thing in the daylight, but she was pretty guarded when it came to talking about herself. She was in a complete mess. It seemed she had been living rough for some time and she had broken up with some bloke and she had been messing around with drugs, too. She had no money at all and the only possession she seemed to care about was her little black jacket. She said she begged a lot. Then she admitted she had been working round King's Cross, selling herself for twenty pounds.

1 How old is Sharon, do you think?
2 What kind of character is she?
3 How does she feel living on the street?
4 How does she relate to other people?
5 How dependent is she on other people?
6 Is she the kind of person who can survive on the street?

Information gap activities Student C

Topic 5: Unit 10, Task 3 (p. 34)

Student C: Read your text and with another C-student answer the following questions. Take individual notes.

1 What is the child most scared of?
2 How does she react towards the daily TV news?
3 To what extent does the child like being scared?
4 When does the child feel most secure?

Katie, aged 12:

I never watch the news intentionally, just sometimes because it comes after 'Neighbours'. I don't want to watch things about people being killed. So I sometimes go out of the room if the news is on or when we're talking about these things. Being frightened is, like, if I'm by myself – and our house is really old – and I hear noises and stuff. I often think there's someone behind me, I get extremely terrified that someone's following me – a murderer! I think more about murderers now – when I was little it was about monsters. I sometimes think about things happening to my parents, but I'm not frightened that it'll really happen. If I've been watching the X-Files or reading horror books before going to bed, then I'm going to be scared, too.

Now, form A/B/C groups and compare your answers with the help of your notes only. What do the three children have in common?

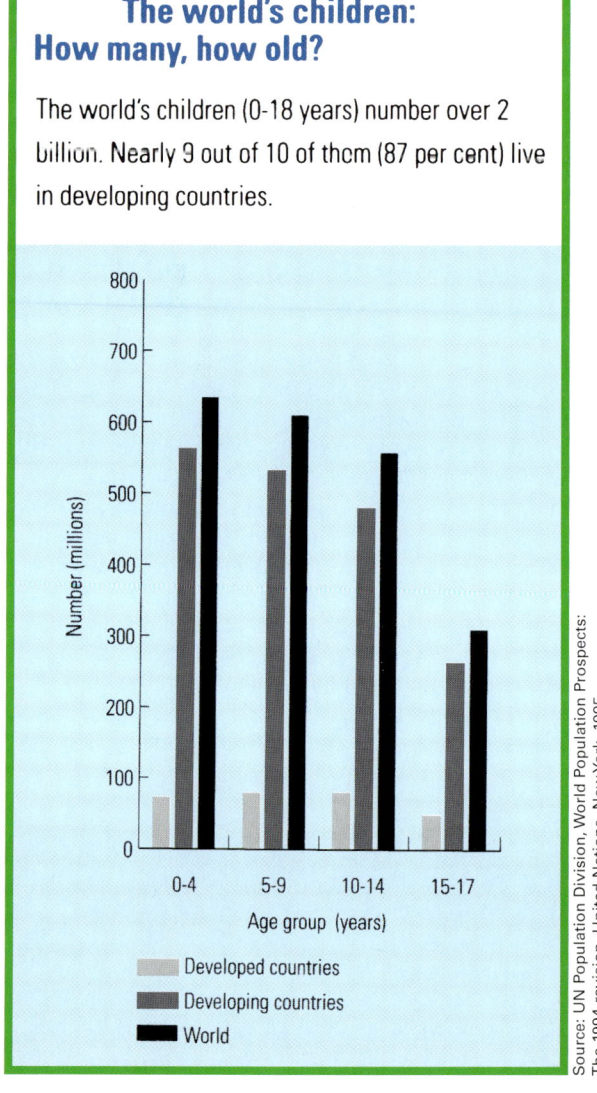

Chart 1

The world's children: How many, how old?

The world's children (0-18 years) number over 2 billion. Nearly 9 out of 10 of them (87 per cent) live in developing countries.

Number (millions) — Age group (years)

- Developed countries
- Developing countries
- World

Source: UN Population Division, World Population Prospects: The 1994 revision, United Nations, New York, 1995.

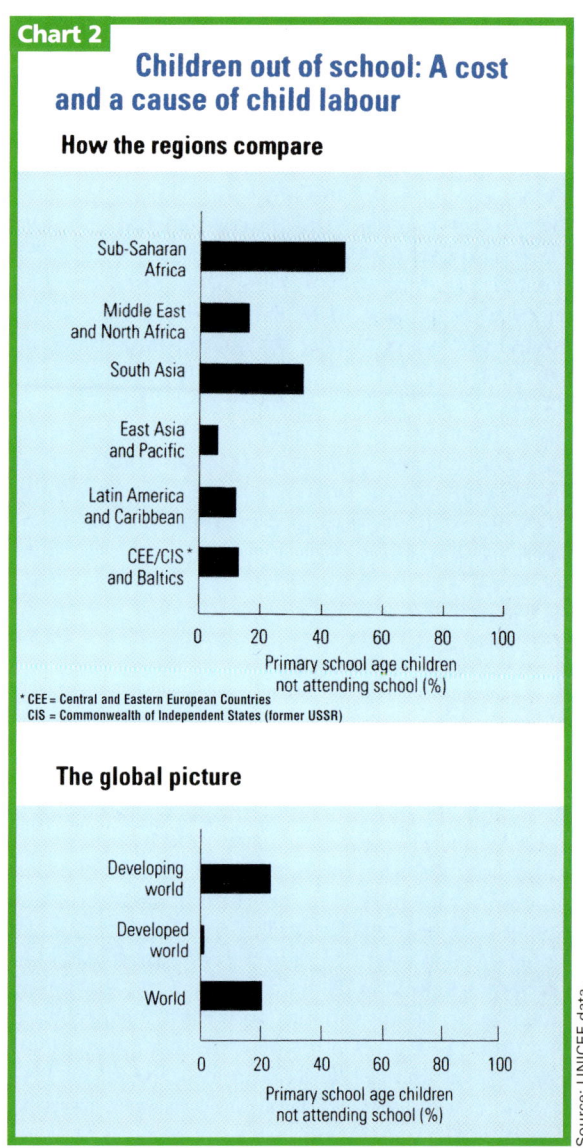

Chart 2

Children out of school: A cost and a cause of child labour

How the regions compare

Sub-Saharan Africa
Middle East and North Africa
South Asia
East Asia and Pacific
Latin America and Caribbean
CEE/CIS* and Baltics

Primary school age children not attending school (%)

* CEE = Central and Eastern European Countries
CIS = Commonwealth of Independent States (former USSR)

The global picture

Developing world
Developed world
World

Primary school age children not attending school (%)

Source: UNICEF data.

79

Cultural information

Topic 1: Activity reading 1 (p. 43)
Ernest Hemingway
American writer (1898-1961)

Some of his short stories reveal Hemingway in his most characteristic mood, illustrating particularly his fascination with the violent side of man's nature. He included violence, brutality, passion, blood, and death in his short stories. Yet for all their harsh reality, his works are also characterized by romance, compassion, and heroic pathos. As a journalist he had learned to develop a very realistic style of writing, reducing his descriptions of actions to a kind of verbal photography. He formed short sentences with strong and simple words and became the envy of a whole school of imitators. But very few managed to convey the compassion that lies between the lines of the simple dialogues and realistic descriptions in Hemingway's stories. 'The Cat in the Rain' is an example of his impressive style of writing.

Topic 2: Activity reading 2 (p. 46)
The Aborigines
The English name for the Native Australians is Aborigines. They were the very first immigrants and came to Australia at least 40,000 years ago. Although the Dutch seafarer Willem Jansz anchored off the north of Queensland in 1606, it was the English sailor James Cook who officially 'discovered' and landed in Australia in 1770. His reports were the signal for settlement by the first Europeans, and up to 1868 about 168,000 convicted prisoners were deported from England and Ireland to Australia. In January 1901 Queen Victoria proclaimed the 'Commonwealth of Australia'. It was only in 1967 that the Aborigines finally got the right to vote. In 1971 the first Aborigine was elected to the state parliament of Queensland. Of the 17 million Australian inhabitants, there are only about 170,000 Aborigines, about 90,000 of whom are half-castes. According to law, the white population and the Aborigines are equal, but the Aborigines still have difficulties adapting to modern civilisation. Cities and houses replace the bushland and they feel helpless in the face of western civilisation and modern technology. On the one hand, the Aborigines living in towns and cities are barely accepted by modern society, on the other hand, they are rejected by their tribesmen who still live in their traditional reservation camps. Like all Nomadic people, the Aborigines have always lived in tribes and are part of nature; private property is unknown to them and time has a different meaning. Some missionaries and scientists discovered that despite their poverty and obviously disorganised lifestyle, Aborigines had a rich culture in which traditions and mythical stories are passed on from generation to generation.

Maureen Watson
Aboriginal storyteller and poet

Maureen Watson is an extraordinarily gifted Murri storyteller who grew up in Queensland. She has five sons and twenty-four grand-children who all have mythical Aborigine names. Anybody who has had the chance to meet Maureen must be fascinated both by her resolute manner and her impressive voice. It is the spoken word which she uses to transmit conviction and the belief in women's and human rights. She has performed in one-woman theatre shows and stage plays both for children and adults. She has given guest lectures at most Australian universities, the Common-wealth Institute in London, Kent University and the University of Nijmegen in Holland. Maureen has appeared in videos, movies, television plays, and has performed in various theatres, including the Sydney Opera House.

Readers: Growing up in a Multicultural Society, A Postcolonial Experience, Nine American Short Stories (original text), Stories from Africa (original text), Stories of the American South (original text), all Langenscheidt-Longman

Topic 3: Activity reading 3 (p. 49)
Kate Chopin
American writer (1851-1904)

In the late 19th and early 20th centuries, the English novel showed two distinct tendencies, each of which represents a reaction to the ideas and values of the Victorian era. The first of these tendencies was moti-vated by the desire to bring back the spirit of romance to the novel, trying to escape from the limitations of stuffy realism. The writers of the second major move-ment regarded the novel as a social document. Their aim was to represent the life of their time, not only accurately but critically. The American historical novels and particularly the native homeland novels (*Heimat-roman*) of the late 19th century are known for their rather romantic characteristics, where life is portrayed as a series of complicated personal relationships, family disputes, stolen inheritances and threefold love stories. In contrast to the poetic atmosphere and the sensitivity of the characters in these novels, Kate Chopin created realistic short stories, in which Guy de Maupassant's work (1850-1893, French realist and naturalist) served as a classic example. The sensuality that pervades the work of Kate Chopin surprises us with its modernity. She makes human emotions come instantly and dramatically alive, which can clearly be felt in 'The Story of an Hour'.

Reader: British and American Short Stories (simplified version: 2000 words), Langenscheidt-Longman

Topic 4: Unit 8, Task 4 (p. 29)
▶ **Voluntary Service Overseas (VSO)**

For thousands of young people the 'gap' year is becoming increasingly popular both before university and afterwards before taking up work. The Community Service Volunteers (CSV) say that the numbers of young people volunteering to help others both in Britain and abroad have increased rapidly.

In the past the Voluntary Service Overseas (VSO) organisation used to send school-leavers to work overseas. However, VSO now normally requires its volunteers not only to be well qualified but to have some experience in the world of work. VSO also organises an Overseas Training Programme which combines ten months spent working in an overseas project which is linked to the student's academic course, together with another two months spent working with organisations in Britain to provide research information and teaching packs on education in various developing countries. Air fares, medical care, training, insurance, and accommodation are provided as part of the scheme.

If you would like more information about VSO, write to: Voluntary Service Overseas, 317 Putney Bridge Road, London SW15 2PN. Tel. 0044 81 780 2266

Reader: Round the World in Eighty Days (simplified version: 2000 words), Langenscheidt-Longman

Topic 5: Activity reading 5 (p. 53)
▶ **Aldous Huxley**
English writer (1894-1963)

The tremendous problems created for Britain by the First World War paved the way for new theories of the state and society. The experience of the Second World War was even more catastrophic than that during the First World War, because in this conflict not only the military forces but also the civilian population were involved. Aldous Huxley was deeply convinced that modern man and society were in a dangerous state. His reaction to the situation tended to be negative or only slightly positive. Huxley's understanding of life and its problems was intellectual and he was primarily critical. His novels showed a reaction of dislike to the moral and spiritual chaos of the modern world. The novels he wrote in the thirties, *Brave New World* (1932), *Eyeless in Gaza* (1936), and *After Many a Summer* (1939), were a series of attempts to find some positive faith that might lead him and his readers out of the labyrinth in which they were lost. Contrary to his grandfather's belief that science would create a new and better world, Huxley protested against the potential destruction of all human values by a society completely controlled by technology. In his later novels he asks for passive resistance to the world's violence and for a life free from desire. He continued to be obsessed with speculations as to the future of mankind. In *Brave New World Revisited* (1958) he showed that many of the fantastic prophecies he had made in *Brave New World* had come true and predicted a society quite as grim as he had forecast earlier. Although published in 1932, this fascinating and at the same time depressing vision of Huxley's 'brave new world' seems to be more relevant to our society today than it has ever been before.

Reader: Brave New World (3000 words and original text), George Orwell: Animal Farm (original text), both Langenscheidt-Longman

Topic 6: Unit 11, Task 7 (p. 39)
▶ **Charles Dickens**
English writer (1812-1870)

Charles Dickens has always been one of the most striking figures in the history of English literature, on account of the dramatic nature of his success. He started from the humblest position in life; when he was ten years old, he worked in a factory, sleeping beneath a counter and spending his Sundays with his family in Marshalsea Prison, where his father was imprisoned for debt. Yet before he was thirty, he was a great writer, and before he was forty, a notable public figure. In middle-age, Dickens began to give semi-dramatic public readings from his works and these grew to be his main interest. He began his career as a reporter, writing sketches of London life for various newspapers. He was later an editor of magazines, and even, for a short time, of a well-known daily newspaper.

One type of character that Dickens developed in his novels, and which in his time made him immensely popular, was that of the victim of society – usually a child. He brought children into the very centre of the action and made them highly individual (Oliver Twist, David Copperfield). For Dickens, the private cruelty which his bad characters cause is almost always connected with social injustice. In nearly all his books there is an attack upon some legal or social evil, which was partly based on the memory of his own bitter childhood. *A Tale of Two Cities* is one of his most powerful novels and deals with the beginnings of industrialisation and the industrial society. It is a remarkable example of his later works.

Simplified readers: David Copperfield (1800 words), Oliver Twist (1800 words), A Tale of Two Cities (2000 words), Hard Times (2500 words) Oliver Twist (3000 words), Great Expectations (3000 words), all Langenscheidt-Longman
Further reader: Outstanding Short Stories by British writers (2000 words), Langenscheidt-Longman

Topic 6: Activity reading 6 (p. 57)
▶ **The Big Issue**

The Big Issue is a magazine by and about homeless people in England where it was first sold in 1991. It was Gordon Roddick (husband of Body Shop millionairess, Anita Roddick) who imported the idea from New York where he had first bought the magazine *Street News*. *The Big Issue* has a circulation of 250,000 copies a week and is sold by 7,000 trained salespeople on the streets of most big towns in Britain. 60 % of the price goes to the homeless salesperson and 40 % goes back to the magazine or to pay for job-training projects for the unemployed. *The Big Issue* organisation has a self-help programme called the *Big Step* which gives practical support and information to their salespeople who want to re-train or who have ideas for their own businesses. Influenced by the success of *The Big Issue*, many European cities have copied the idea and are selling their own issues now, like *La Rue* in Paris, *Terre di mezzo* in Italy and *Biss* in Munich.

Reader: The Human Element and Other Stories (original text), Langenscheidt-Longman

English on the Internet – a few tips

To use the *Internet* first you need a *computer* with the relevant *software* and an *Internet* connection. Information in the *Internet* can be found on the so-called *homepage* provided by each contributor (newspapers, large firms, TV companies and organisations or individual people). You can identify and locate any *homepage* with the help of a *search engine* (available in your *Internet* software) or if you already know the exact *homepage address* by typing it in. (It usually begins with http://www.)

Using addresses in the Internet you can

• **get into contact with English speakers** all over the world and write or talk to them directly via *E-Mail* or *Voice-Mail*.

• **join in communications** within the so-called *Chat-Groups* of the *Usenet*. Here you can read what other people have said about certain topics and add your own opinion. Or you can start your own enquiry and ask people to contact you.

• **read and study texts** from the latest editions of English newspapers and magazines. By choosing the *homepage* of *The Times* or the *Guardian*, for example, you can find and print out articles that interest you.

• **find out more about books and their authors**. You can look for the name of an author (via a *search engine*), e.g. Aldous Huxley, or the title of a book and read commentaries, reviews, background information etc., or find the addresses of international booksellers where you can order the book. If there's an *e-mail address* on the *homepage,* then you can sometimes contribute your own opinion.

• **discover** independently from your course work more **background information** about any topic you choose, e.g. about the British Royal Family on the Buckingham Palace *homepage*.

• **investigate** the work done by **large organisations** in the English-speaking world, e.g. NASA, whose *homepage* contains numerous articles on the exploration of space.

• find out what **language courses** are available in the English-speaking countries, e.g. in Britain via the British Council *homepage*.

• **make plans for your holidays**. If you wanted, for example, to visit somewhere like Fowey in Cornwall this year, you could call up a list of hotels, events, sights, opening times, travel facilities etc.

If you don't have an Internet connection at home but would still like to have access to the information, why not call in at an *Internet-Café*? These now exist in a lot of places. You can go along, work on the *Internet* and just pay for what you use.

Here are a few very useful *homepage* addresses:

The Times (UK):	http://www.the-times.co.uk
BBC (UK):	http://www.bbc.co.uk
TIME Magazine (US):	http://pathfinder.com/time
CNN (US):	http://www.cnn.com
The New York Times (US):	http://www.nytimesfax.com
National Geographic (US):	http://www.nationageographic.com
Victoria & Albert Museum (UK):	http://www.vam.ac.uk
Encyclopedia Britannica (UK):	http://www.eb.com
British Tourist Authority (UK):	http://www.bta.org.uk
The British Council	http://www.britcoun.org
Roget's Thesaurus	http://www2.thesaurus.com
The Library of Congress (US):	http://lcweb.loc.gov.
Langenscheidt-Longman Verlag	http://www.langlong.de

A lot of *homepage* addresses will provide "links" to other sources worldwide. Have fun "surfing"!

Remember: the *Internet* is constantly being changed and addresses cannot be guaranteed indefinitely.

Grammar

This grammar review focuses mainly on the three tenses of the verb (A), the present (1), the past (2) and the future (3), as they form the basis for conditionals, passive forms and reported speech.

Furthermore, this review includes a separate summary of each the progressive forms (B), the conditionals (C) and the passives (D) and considers the change of tenses in reported speech (E). There is a network of cross-references to be consulted if necessary. The arrows in each section indicate the corresponding section or part, e.g. Section: Tenses, present progressive: She is having an interview tomorrow. → progressive forms, → future. The examples which illustrate each of the grammar points are predominantly taken from the texts in this book in order to illustrate the grammar rules by means of a context known to you. The numbers added to the examples refer to the corresponding unit, e.g. 3/5 = Unit 3, task 5. If you would like to study the grammar in more detail, you could use these books: *English Network Grammar* (ISBN 50 412-1) and *Longman English Grammar Practice* (ISBN 04 500-3).

A The tenses

1 Talking about the present

The present simple is used
• to talk about actions and situations which repeatedly happen, all the time or at any time (always, sometimes, never, usually, frequently, often, once in a while, nowadays):

My mum and dad phone me regularly. 1/7
I always get up at seven in the morning.

• to talk about habitual and general facts:

I generally try to make an effort. 1/7

• to express feelings and senses:

Nowadays, I feel much more content.

• to express a mental state (think, believe, know, remember):

Baysee thinks that musicians are terrible eaters. 1/6   → reported speech

• in an *if*-clause (conditional 1):

If you eat too much, you'll get fat.
→ conditionals

• in a (present) time clause with *when* or *whenever*:

I always feel happy when I go on holiday. 1/2

• to talk about scheduled events:

The train leaves at ten past seven.   → future

The present progressive is used
• to talk about actions and situations which are going on at the time of speaking:

Compare:
Rebecca is still living on her own.
(for the moment) 5/4   → progressive forms
Baysee lives on his own in Leyton.
(fact / all the time) 1/6

• to talk about actions that happen regularly or often and which are annoying the speaker (always, constantly, continually, forever):

Compare:
He is always parking his car in front of the house.
(It's annoying me.)
He always parks his car in front of the house.
(It's a fact.)

• to talk about future plans (including a time word):

Compare:
What are you doing on Sunday? (at a fixed time in the future)   → future
What are you doing here? (at the moment)
What do you do? (What's your job?)

The modal verbs *may, must, could, might* and *should* are used with the present
• to express degrees of certainty or uncertainty or to make assumptions:

Compare: → modal verbs with present perfect
Kim must be a very courageous person.
(almost certain)
She should be back from her holiday by now.
(fairly certain)
Jane could / may be married.
(fairly certain) – (**not:** It could be that …)
He might be a millionaire.
(fairly uncertain) – (**not:** It is possible that he …)

2 Talking about the past

The present perfect simple
It is difficult to place the present perfect tense. It does not really belong to the past, as it relates a past action with a present situation and expresses more about the present situation than the past. It is used
• to express actions and situations continuing up to the present which are either not completed or not over yet. (yet / not yet, already, still, ever (?), never, since / for, so far, lately, recently, all my life, up to now):

Compare:
I have been angry for a long time. (until now and I still am)
I was angry for a long time. (then, but not now)
→ past simple

• to talk about a finished past action or to report facts and news of past events where the present result is more important than the time of action:

I have just washed the car. (It's clean now.)

Compare:
Look, I have had my hair cut. (I have been to the hairdresser's.)
Look, I have cut my hair. (I've done it myself.)

The present perfect progressive is used
• to talk about an action which started in the past and may or may not be completed at the time of speaking; it emphasises the continuation of the activity:

Ellen has been living in an old people's home. (until now and still is) 5/4   → progressive forms
How long has she been living there? (emphasis on the length of time) For ten years. / Since 1990.
How many friends has she made? (emphasis on the number of friends)

The past simple is used
• to talk about actions and situations of a point or period of time which is now over or which happened at a given time in the past (yesterday, last month):

When I first saw my grand-daughter, I felt the purest love. 1/2

• to talk about unfulfilled present conditions:

I wish / If only I had more time. (but I don't)
→ conditionals

• to report what someone said / believed about a present action or situation:

Teachers said that Ruth worked hard and was a very ambitious student.   → reported speech

Would in place of the past simple is used
• when we remember or refer to moments of the past or talk about past habits:

When I was at school, everybody would say to me "School days are the best days of your life." 3/6

Used to in place of the past simple is used
• to refer to past habits when we want to make a contrast between the past and the present, expressing *but not any more / not any longer:*

Compare:
Jane used to hate school. (but not any more) 4/3
I was / got used to taking exams. (I was/got accustomed to it.)   → ing-forms and infinitives

The past progressive is used
• to talk about temporary actions which were in progress in the past:

I didn't see very much of my own children when they were growing up. 1/2   → progressive forms

• to talk about actions which were in progress when something else happened:

Traffic was moving at a normal speed when a lorry came to a sudden stop. LiA/6

The past perfect is used
• to refer to an action which happened before a moment in the past and was completed *then:*

Ruth forgot everything she had learnt during the previous two years. 4/7

• to talk about impossible, unfulfilled or unlikely past actions:

If I had spent a year travelling, I would have stayed away from the tourists. 8/4   → conditionals

• to report what someone said about a past action or situation:

> He told me that he had worked hard the previous day. → reported speech

The past perfect progressive is used
• to emphasise the continuity of an action which started before a moment in the past and lasted until that very moment, or even longer:

> It felt as if I had been learning for ever. 1/2 → progressive forms

The modal verb forms *could, would, might, should* **and** *must* are also used with the present perfect
• to talk about possible actions or situations of the past:

> I could have bought a house for very little money, but I didn't. 2/4 → conditionals
> A 'gap year' would / might have given me more perspective on life. 8/4 → conditionals

• to express assumptions:

> Compare: → modal verbs with the present
> James must have had a very early start in his career. 4/4 (almost certain)
> Ruth should / could have recovered from her accident by now. (fairly certain)
> He might have won in the lottery. (very uncertain)

The future-in-the-past is used
• to refer to events we (at one time in the past) believed would happen (or not) in the future, or to events we couldn't foresee:

> I knew instinctively that TV was going to be something huge. 2/4 → reported speech

3 Talking about the future

This future section focuses mainly on the future tenses with *will*. *Will*-constructions include the future simple, the future progressive, the future perfect and the future perfect progressive.

There are, however, four ways of forming the 'future simple' in English. Three of them use present tense constructions (1–3). In order to differentiate between the different forms, it is important to consider the speaker's attitude as much as the certainty and time of the arrangement.

Compare:
1 The plane **takes off** at 19.00 hours. (scheduled or regular 'time-tabled' events) → present simple
2 I**'m travelling** to London tomorrow. (planned or already arranged) → present progressive
3 I**'m going to travel** to London tomorrow. (planned and intended)
4 I**'ll take** you to the airport. (spontaneous offer/ instant decision)
I**'ll probably travel** to London next week. (not certain)
I suppose we**'ll live / be living** in skyscrapers in the future. (prediction)

The future simple with *will* is used
• to make predictions or to express what we think will happen:

> The Internet global network will allow you to work anywhere. 11/2
> If they want to be successful, the organisers will need to create a sense of identity. 11/3 → conditionals

The future progressive with *will* is used
• to express an action which starts at a given time in the future and will probably continue after that (emphasis on length of time):

> Once people move in, they will soon be missing busy city life. 11/2 → progressive forms

• to say that someone will be in the middle of doing something at a given time in the future:

> They will still be renovating the houses when the first occupants move in.

• to talk about something already planned with emphasis on the length of time, similar to the present progressive:

> The future inhabitants will be holding video conferences with offices around the world. 11/2

The future perfect is used
• to talk about an action which will have been finished or which will already have happened before a certain time in the future:

> Compare:
> People will have moved in **by** the end of this year. (the last possible point)
> **But**: People will be able to buy a house **until** the end of this year. (emphasis on how long)

The future perfect progressive is used
• to emphasise the length of time an action will have lasted by a point of time in the future:

> Next year I will have been living in this town for 30 years. (… and will continue to live here.)
> → progressive forms

B The progressive forms

The progressive forms are used
• to talk about an action or situation that is, was, has / had been going on, will be / will have been or would be / would have been going on at a certain moment that we are thinking about.
• to emphasise that actions are temporary or incomplete.

> Compare:
> He **is travelling** through Europe. (at the moment)
> → present progressive
> He **is leaving** tonight.
> (planned) → future
> He **has been travelling** for a long time.
> (and still is) → present perfect progressive
> He **was visiting** Paris when I met him. (at that very moment) → past progressive
> He **had been studying** languages before taking a year off. → past perfect progressive
> He **will be travelling** to the USA soon.
> → future progressive
> He **could / should / might be travelling** with a friend. → conditionals → modals

> He **will have been travelling** for a year next August. → future perfect progressive
> He **could / should / might have been working** in Paris. → conditionals → modals
> He **is being observed** by the police. (now)
> → present progressive passive
> He **was being observed** by the police. (yesterday)
> → past progressive passive

Different meanings (simple/progressive)
When using the progressive forms, the difference between 'stative' and 'dynamic' verbs has to be considered. 'Stative' verbs don't (or rarely) take the progressive form, e.g. *I like languages*. With 'dynamic' verbs, the person is actively doing something, e.g. *I'm writing a letter.*

> a) I feel great! (stative)
>   I'm feeling rather tired. (dynamic)
> b) She has a new car. (stative)
>   She is having lots of fun. (dynamic)
> c) I think grammar is confusing at times. (stative)
>   I'm thinking about changing my job. (dynamic)

C Conditionals

The first conditional is used
• to talk about a possible present condition and to look from the present into the future. In the *if*-clause, all present and future tenses can be used:
> → present → future

> **If** children start putting their money to work now, they will / can / may / are going to make far more from it than if they start at 40. 2/7
> **Provided** the programme is interesting, I even accept package tours. 7/2
> **Unless** you join me, I won't go. (= If you don't)

> Compare:
> I'll visit you **when** I'm in town. (I don't know when exactly.)
> I'll visit you **if** I'm in town. (I don't know whether I'll go there.)

The second conditional is used
• to talk about an impossible or unlikely present (not past) condition: → past simple

> I wouldn't / couldn't enjoy a package holiday if it was luxurious. 7/2
> Provided (that) / If I had enough money, I would travel in great comfort.
> **I wish / If only** I had a year to spend with nothing much to do. 8/3
> If I were you, I'd take a year off. (giving advice: **not**: If I was …)

The third conditional is used
• to talk about an unfulfilled or unknown past condition: → past perfect → perfect modal verbs

> Provided / If money had been no object, I might / would have gone in a Land Rover. 8/4
> I wish / If only I could have gone abroad. 8/4

> Compare:
> If I hadn't gone abroad, I wouldn't have made so many friends. (then)
> If I hadn't gone abroad, I would regret it. (now)

D The passive

The passive forms are used
- to emphasise the event rather than who or what did it. We use *by* only when we want to say who or what is responsible for the action:

Women who stay at home **are made** to feel like second-class citizens. 3/2
→ present simple

The kidnapper **is being interviewed** by the police. → present progressive

Another kidnapping **has been reported** today. 10/8 → present perfect simple

The police in Ireland **were** later **warned**. 10/9
→ past simple

Mrs Davies **had been informed** straight after the discovery of her baby. 10/9
→ past perfect

The kidnapper **will** probably **be taken** to court. 10/9 → future simple

Within a few years, more skyscrapers **will have been built**. → future perfect

Compare:
She has been called by the police.
→ present perfect passive
She has been calling the police several times.
→ present perfect progressive

The passive with modal verbs

Any findings by the public **should / might be reported**. 10/8 → modal verbs
Nicola **should / could have been given** better care. → modal verbs with present perfect

Infinitive construction after passive verbs like say, believe, know, consider, mean, agree, decide, expect, suppose:

I'm said / believed / known / considered to be well-mannered and reliable. 6/5
Work was thought to be the most effective way of teaching children about life. 12/6
Children are expected to give their entire wages to their parents. 12/6

E Reported speech

Reported statements
The most common reporting verbs are *say (to s.o.), tell (s.o.)* and *ask (s.o.)*. Other reporting verbs are, for example, *explain, remark, reveal, mention, believe, think, argue, admit, claim, criticise, be convinced, shout, whisper.* In continuous reports, we can use phrases like: *He continued, saying that ... , She added that ... , They went on to say that ... .*

If we quote an immediate statement and use the reporting verb in the present simple or in the present perfect, no change of tense is required in the reported clause. But as we mostly refer to past events when reporting, the reporting verb is often used in the past. In this case, we generally change the tense in the reported sentence by moving it back in time: present → past, past → past perfect.

"We find that TV **provides** better discussions."
→ Parents argued that TV **provided** better discussions. 9/6

present simple
past simple

"TV **is getting** worse."
→ She said that TV **was getting** worse.

present progressive
past progressive

"We are convinced that TV **has improved**."
→ They were convinced that TV **had improved**. 9/6

present perfect
past perfect

"I **didn't see** the film last night."
→ He told us he **hadn't seen** the film the previous night.

past simple
past perfect

"I **was watching** TV when the phone rang."
→ She explained that she **had been watching** TV when the phone rang.

past progressive
past perfect progressive

"We **will never give up** our TV."
→ They admitted that they **would never give up** their TV.

future simple with *will*
would

"I don't think I**'m going to watch** this film."
→ She didn't think she **was going to watch** that film.

going to-future
future in the past

"You **couldn't live** without a TV."
→ He believed that I **couldn't live** without a TV. (no change of tense!)

→ modal verbs

"You **should have taken** a holiday, John."
→ Sue told John he **should have taken** a holiday. (no change!)

→ modal verbs with present perfect

Reported questions

When reporting a question, verbs like *ask, wonder, want to know, inquire, be curious to know if /* *whether* are used. If the verb is used in the past, we change the reported question one tense back as shown on page 87.

"Where **are** the role models on children's television?"
➜ They wondered where the role models on children's television **were**. 9/6

⎰ present simple
⎱ past simple

Reported requests, orders, offers, promises used with infinitive

"Can / Could / Would you help me, please?"   ➜ He asked / requested / wanted me to help him.
"Don't forget to call me."   ➜ He told / reminded me not to forget to call him.
"Come on, I'll give you a hand."   ➜ He offered / promised to give me a hand.

F *ing*-forms and infinitives

Gerund as a noun, e.g. swimming, working, reading:

Playing in a team can improve your social life. 5/8

• ***-ing*-form after preposition**, e.g. what about, without, by, against, after, before, besides, like:

After spending five days in intensive care, Ruth made quite a dramatic recovery. 4/7

• ***-ing*-form after noun + preposition**, e.g. a chance of, difficulty in, a danger of, hope of, no point in, an excuse for, a need for, a talent for:

I've never been a great believer in investing in shares. 2/3

• ***-ing*-form after verb**, e.g. admit, deny, avoid, consider, imagine, can't resist, can't help, keep, miss, mind, risk, go, resent, like, love, enjoy, appreciate, dislike, welcome, prefer, hate, can't stand:

I couldn't imagine doing anything different. 4/4

• ***-ing*-form after verb + preposition**, e.g. care about, count on, disapprove of, dream about, escape from, keep away from, feel like, use for, give up, know about, apologise for, think of, talk about, worry about, look forward to, prevent s.o. from, forgive s.o. for:

Ruth's parents insisted on her going to university.

• ***-ing*-form after adjective**, e.g. worth, nice, busy, great:

I was always so busy working. 1/2

• ***-ing*-form after adjective + preposition**, e.g. bothered about, annoyed about, bored with, sorry for, crazy about, (un)happy about, afraid of, tired of, fond of, enthusiastic about, interested in, proud of, good at, serious about, keen on, be used to:

James was very talented at organising parties. 4/4

Verb + *-ing*-form or infinitive

• The *-ing*-form refers to the past, the infinitive to what happens after:

Compare:
I clearly remember sitting my exams. 3/6
(I have it clearly in my mind.)
I should remember to buy the book.
(I shouldn't forget.)
I've never regretted going to university. 4/4
(I've never felt sorry about going there.)
I regret to inform / tell you that … .
(I would rather not.)
Ruth will never forget spending weeks in hospital.
(forget what has happened to her.)
He always forgets to lock the door.
(He forgets what he has to do.)
She stopped smoking last year.
(She doesn't smoke any more.)
She stopped her work to smoke a cigarette.
(in order to smoke a cigarette.)

• The *-ing*-form refers to general facts, the infinitive to a specific event or intention:

Compare:
I prefer doing sports to walking. (in general)
I'd prefer to go for a walk today. (on this special occasion)
I like visiting people. (I generally enjoy it.)
I wouldn't like to visit him but I'll have to. (I would rather not this time.)

Infinitive after verb, e.g. afford, expect, promise, agree, appear, ask, help, hope, intend, dare (without 'to'!), fail, hesitate, refuse, arrange, learn, offer, pretend, seem, tend, try, want, decide, manage:

Working mothers tend to be organised. 3/2

The meaning of a word is the way it is used in the context. When looking up a word in a dictionary, you should always keep in mind that a correct definition for a word is only possible in connection with its place in the sentence. Because of the variety of meanings you have to look at the surrounding words which may indicate the possible meaning of the word in question, e.g.: She's very *kind*. (helpful, caring, friendly) – What *kind* of car has she got? (group with its own character) – She *kind* of hoped to be invited. (in a way, infml) He spoke to her angrily and she replied in *kind*. (with the same treatment)

Although using a bilingual dictionary (English/German) seems to be less time-consuming, a monolingual dictionary (English/English) undoubtedly offers more opportunities to expand on vocabulary. With almost every word you look up, you get to know synonyms or examples that carry the same or a similar meaning as the word in question. In some dictionaries, for example the new *Longman Active Study Dictionary of English*, you get even further information: Important words are marked to help you learn and remember them, and grammar notes at the foot of every fourth page provide helpful reminders about difficult points of grammar. Using a dictionary creates interest and is therefore a challenge in itself. If you like, find the answers to the following questions with the help of your dictionary, for example the *Longman Active Study Dictionary of English*. You will find the answer in the key that follows.

► Dictionaries help with pronunciation, word stress and spelling.

1 Look up the pronunciation of: a) *class* and *glass*, b) *few* and *view*, c) *share* and *chair*, d) *think* and *sink*. What is the difference in each pair?

2 Which of these two words is stressed on the first syllable? *photograph / photographer*

3 Which of the two versions of the word *address* (the stressed syllable is printed in bold) is American, which is British? a) **a**ddress, b) addr**ess**

4 What's the American spelling of *honour*?

► Dictionaries support you when you have grammar problems.

5 What do these abbreviations (in **bold** print) mean? *impress **v**, impression **n**, impressive **adj**, impressively **adv**, get on **phr v**, money **U**, news **sing**, police **pl***

6 Look up the word *difficulty*. Which is correct: I have difficulties a) to understand, b) understanding, c) in understanding a word.

7 What is the past tense of the verb *seek*?

8 Which is correct: a) There are all *kind* of learners. b) There are all *kinds* of learners. (see Usage of *kind*)

9 Which of these words are countable? *furniture, information, fruit, vegetable, money, cash, note, news, advice, change*

10 How many different grammatical forms (adj, adv, n, v,) does each of these words have? *exercise, clean, colour*

► Dictionaries help you to discover more about the language you are learning.

Phrasal Verbs
In English there are many verbs which are made up of two or three words. These are called 'phrasal verbs'. Phrasal verbs may have a completely different meaning from the main verb. They can be found after the entry for the main verb, like this:

> **dry**² *v* [I,T] to become dry, or to make something dry: *It'll only take me a few minutes to dry my hair* —**dried** *adj*: *dried fruit*
> **dry off** *phr v* [I,T **dry** sth ↔ **off**] to become dry or make the surface of something dry: *The kids played in the pool and then dried off in the sun.*

11 Look up the word *brief*. How many different meanings can you find? Is there a verb?

12 List words that are related to *horror*.

13 Find the words related to *create*.

14 How many phrasal verbs can you find with the verb *bring*, e.g. *bring along sthg/sbdy*?

► Dictionaries help you with questions of usage.

Words which are often confused
Usage Notes give you more information about words and how to use them, and words which are often confused. They often show alternative words too. Look at this Usage Note about the word **affect**.

> **af·fect** /əˈfekt/ *v* [T] **1** to cause a change in someone or something or to change the situation they are in: *a disease that affects the heart and lungs* | *Help is being sent to areas affected by the floods.* **2** to make someone feel strong emotions: *She was deeply affected by the news of Pauls death.* →compare EFFECT²

> **USAGE NOTE: affect and effect**
> **Affect** is always a verb, used to talk about the way one thing changes or influences another: *How will the new law affect young people?* **Effect** is a noun, meaning what happens as a result of a change or influence: *What effect will the new law have?* **Effect**, however, is sometimes used as a verb in formal English, meaning to make something happen: *efforts to effect a peaceful solution to the conflict.*

15 Which of the two phrases is American?
a) Let's stay *at home* tonight.
b) Let's stay *home* tonight.
(see Usage of *home*)

16 What's the difference between *entry* and *entrance*? (see Usage of *entrance*)

▶ Dictionaries help you to understand how words are constructed.

Knowing more about the construction of words helps you to understand the meaning of seemingly unknown vocabulary and even enables you to construct or create words yourself which so far you haven't used. For example, prefixes (word beginnings) and suffixes (word endings) give you hints about the type of word.

unexpect**ed**: un- = opposite, -ed = adjective

quick**ly**: -ly = adverb
disconnec**tion**: dis- = opposite, -ion = noun
unjustifi**able**: un- = opposite, -able = adjective
justific**ation**: -ation = noun
justi**fy**: -fy = verb

17 Find adjectives that take the prefix ir-, e.g. irresponsible.
18 Find verbs beginning with over-.

▶ Dictionaries help you to learn about phrases and word combinations.

19 Find compound adjectives beginning with the word good, e.g. good-hearted.
20 Find compound nouns beginning with hair, e.g. hairbrush.

21 Look up the word time. What can you do with time? E.g. waste time.

▶ Dictionaries provide you with the opportunity to develop your language skills further.

You don't necessarily need a vocabulary workbook to expand your vocabulary. All kinds of dictionaries where words are grouped either under a topic or a headword can serve the same purpose and are a helpful tool when writing essays or letters. Or they might just offer you a pleasant hour of detective work without a specific aim.

If you look up the word happy in the Longman Language Activator for example, you can find various expressions for different kinds of feeling of happiness,

e.g. cheerful, be in a good mood, content, be on top of the world, etc. In the Longman Lexicon, another vocabulary source book, there are a number of verbs related to the word pleasure, like enjoy, please, gladden, delight etc.

As you can see, there's more to a dictionary than just finding out about the meaning of a specific word. It can be great fun to 'surf' through the pages and to do a detour sometimes, finding out about other directions and areas, too. So, enjoy working with your dictionary!

Key to Dictionary skills

1 a) /klɑːs/ /glɑːs/   b) /fjuː/ /vjuː/   c) /ʃeəʳ/ /tʃeəʳ/
d) /θɪŋk/ /sɪŋk/
2 photograph /ˈfəʊtəgrɑːf/   photograph /fəˈtɒgrəfəʳ/
3 a) American /ˈædres/ b) British /əˈdres/
4 honor
5 v = verb, n = noun, adj = adjective, adv = adverb, phr v = phrasal verb, U = uncountable, sing = singular, pl = plural
6 I have difficulties in understanding a word. (c)
7 sought
8 There are all kinds of learners. (b)
9 fruit: countable (C [the fruits of = result]) and uncountable (U [We need some more fruit]), vegetables, notes, change (C = There have been a lot of changes. and U = I need some change = money)
10 exercise (n, v), clean (v, adj, adv), colour (n, v)
11 a brief look (not lasting very long), a brief letter (using only a few words), the news in brief (using only a few words), a brief (set of instructions about sbdy's duties), to brief sbdy (give instructions or necessary information to sbdy)
12 horrendous(ly), horrible, horrid(ly), horrific(ally), horrify, horrified, horrifying
13 created, creating, creation, creative(ly), creativity, creativeness, creator
14 bring sthg about, bring (sthg/sbdy) back, bring (sbdy/sthg) down, bring sthg forward, bring (sbdy/sthg) in, bring sthg off, bring (sbdy/sthg) on, bring (sbdy/sthg)

out, bring sbdy round, bring sbdy to, bring (sbdy/sthg) up
15 Let's stay home tonight. (b)
16 For the ordinary act of entering, the usual word is entry: Britain's entry into the EEC. "No entry" (road sign). Entrance is used especially to talk about a ceremony or performance: to make an entrance onto the stage, or to talk about the right to enter: a university entrance exam / an entrance fee. It is also commonly used to describe the way into a large building.
17 irrational, irreconcilable, irrefutable, irregular, irrelevant, irreparable, irreplacable, irrepressible, irreproachable, irresistible, irresponsible, irreverent, irrevocable, irritable
18 overbalance, overcharge, overcome, overcompensate, overdo, overestimate, overflow, overhang, overhaul, overhear, overheat, overlap, overload, overlook, overpower, overrate, override, overrule, overrun, oversee, overshadow, overshoot, oversimplify, oversleep, overstate, overstep, overtake, overthrow, overturn, overwhelm, overwork
19 good-humoured, good-looking, good-natured, good-tempered
20 haircut, hairdo, hairdresser, hairdryer, hairgrip, hairline, hairnet, hairpiece, hairpin, hair's breadth, hair slide, hair-splitting, hairstyle
21 have (no) time, take (your) time, spend/pass/waste time, mark time, make time, lose time, kill time

A

abandoned [ə'bændnd] verlassen, aufgegeben

abandonment [ə'bændənmənt] Hemmungslosigkeit

abuse [ə'bju:z] misshandeln

access ['ækses] Zugang

accompany [ə'kʌmpəni] begleiten

account [ə'kaunt]: **bank account** Bankkonto; **take into account** in Betracht ziehen, berücksichtigen

accuse (s.o. of) [ə'kju:z (əv)] beschuldigen

accustomed (to) [ə'kʌstəmd (tə)] gewöhnt (an)

achievement [ə'tʃi:vmənt] Vollbringung, Leistung

adapted [ə'dæptɪd] bearbeitet *(Text)*

addict ['ædɪkt] Süchtige(r)

additional(ly) [ə'dɪʃənəl(ɪ)] zusätzlich, außerdem

advance [əd'vɑ:ns] vorwärts gehen

adventurous [əd'ventʃərəs] abenteuerlustig

affected (by) [ə'fektɪd (baɪ)] beeinträchtigt, betroffen (von)

afflicted (with) [ə'flɪktɪd (wɪð)] leidend (an), behaftet (mit)

ages ['eɪdʒɪz]: **for ages** eine Ewigkeit lang

agony ['ægəni] Qual, Seelenangst

alcohol-drenched ['ælkəhɒl 'drentʃt] Alkohol getränkt

alert [ə'lɜ:t] rege, munter

alien ['eɪlɪən] außerirdisches Wesen

amazing [ə'meɪzɪŋ] erstaunlich, verblüffend

ambitious [æm'bɪʃəs] ehrgeizig, strebsam

annoyed [ə'nɔɪd] ärgerlich, verärgert

apparent [ə'pærənt]: **become apparent** ersichtlich, klar werden

appreciate [ə'pri:ʃɪeɪt] schätzen, würdigen

appropriate [ə'prəʊprɪət] entsprechend, passend

armed [ɑ:md] bewaffnet

artificial(ly) [ɑ:tɪ'fɪʃəl(ɪ)] künstlich

assumption [ə'sʌmʃn] Annahme, Vermutung

assure (o.s.) [ə'ʃʊə] (sich) überzeugen, vergewissern

attend school [ə,tend 'sku:l] die Schule besuchen

attract attention [ə'trækt ə'tenʃn] die Aufmerksamkeit auf sich ziehen

authoritative [ə'θɒrətətɪv] gebieterisch, herrisch

available [ə'veɪləbl] verfügbar, vorhanden

awareness [ə'weənəs] Bewusstsein, Kenntnis

awkward ['ɔ:kwəd] verlegen

B

back up ['bæk 'ʌp] stärken, unterstützen

bar [bɑ:] Stange, Stab

barrel ['bærəl] (rundes) Gehäuse

basically ['beɪsɪklɪ] grundsätzlich, im Grunde

beaten ['bi:tn]: **off the beaten track** abgelegen

behaviour [bɪ'heɪvjə] Verhalten

bespeak [bɪ'spi:k] zeugen von, zeigen

better-off [,betə'ɒf] wohlhabender, besser situiert

bloke [bləʊk] Kerl

bosom ['bʊzm] Busen

bother ['bɒðə] sich Mühe geben

bothered (about) ['bɒðəd] **be bothered (about)** beunruhigt sein

bow [baʊ] sich verneigen

brand name ['brænd 'neɪm] Markenname

break [breɪk]: **break the news gently to s.o.** jdm. die Nachricht schonend beibringen

breed [bri:d] Stamm, Art

brief [bri:f] kurz

bulging ['bʌldʒɪŋ] (zum Bersten) voll

bull-fighting ['bʊl,faɪtɪŋ] Stierkampf

burden ['bɜ:dən] Last, Bürde

burgle ['bɜ:gl] einbrechen

burst [bɜ:st] (zer)platzen, (auf)springen: **burst with pride** platzen vor Stolz

C

casually (dressed) ['kæʒjʊəlɪ] salopp, sportlich (gekleidet)

celebrate ['selɪbreɪt] ein Fest feiern

celebrity [,se'lebrətɪ] Berühmtheit *(Person)*

challenging ['tʃæləndʒɪŋ] herausfordernd

channel-hopper ['tʃænl ,hɒpə] Programm-, Kanalhüpfer, 'Zapper' *(TV)*

chart [tʃɑ:t] graphische Darstellung

cheek [tʃi:k] Backe, Wange

chief executive [,tʃi:f ɪg'zekjʊtɪv] Leiter(in) *(amer.)*

childminder ['tʃaɪld,maɪndə] Tagesmutter

chin [tʃɪn] Kinn

claim (that) [kleɪm (ðæt)] behaupten (dass)

clasp [klɑ:sp] umklammern, fest ergreifen

classy ['klɑ:sɪ] 'Klasse'

clip [klɪp] (mit der Maschine) schneiden

clot of blood ['klɒt_əv_'blʌd] Blutgerinnsel

comment ['kɒment] Anmerkung, Kommentar

commit crimes [kə,mɪt 'kraɪmz] Verbrechen begehen

commitment [kə'mɪtmənt] Verpflichtung, Bindung

community [kə'mju:nətɪ] Gemeinschaft

commute [kə'mju:t] pendeln

competition [,kɒmpɪ'tɪʃn] Wettbewerb

compose [kəm'pəʊz] komponieren

conclusion [kən'klu:ʒn] (Schluss)Folgerung

concrete ['kɒnkri:t] Beton

condition [kən'dɪʃn] bestimmen, regeln

conductor [kən'dʌktə] (Bus)Schaffner

confess [kən'fes] gestehen, zugeben

confidence ['kɒnfɪdəns] Vertrauen

confidently ['kɒnfɪdəntlɪ] vertrauensvoll, selbstsicher

confused [kən'fju:zd] verwirrt

considerably [kən'sɪdərəblɪ] beträchtlich, erheblich

consideration [kənsɪdə'reɪʃn]: **take into consideration** in Betracht, Erwägung ziehen

constantly ['kɒnstəntlɪ] unaufhörlich, stetig

contentment [kən'tentmənt] Zufriedenheit

conviction [kən'vɪkʃn] Überzeugung

convinced [kən'vɪnsd] überzeugt

correspond (to/with) [kɒrɪ'spɒnd (tə/wɪð)] übereinstimmen (mit), entsprechen

council ['kaʊnsl] Gemeinde

courage ['kʌrɪdʒ] Mut, Tapferkeit

creep [kri:p] kriechen

crouch [kraʊtʃ] (sich zs.) kauern

cruelty ['krʊəltɪ] Grausamkeit

cry [kraɪ] Schrei

curse [kɜ:s] verfluchen, verdammen

cushion ['kʊʃn] Kissen, Polster

D

damn [dæm] verdammen, verwünschen

darn (damn) [dɑ:n (dæm)] verdammt

deal [di:l]: **a great deal** sehr viel

deal [di:l] Handel treiben

Dictionary

debate [dɪˈbeɪt] Debatte, Erörterung
decade [ˈdekeɪd] Jahrzehnt
decrease [dɪˈkriːs] abnehmen, sich vermindern
degree [dɪˈɡriː] Grad, Maß
delicious [dɪˈlɪʃəs] köstlich, herrlich
deliver [dɪˈlɪvə] liefern, zustellen
descend [dɪˈsend] hinuntersteigen
despair [dɪˈspeə] Verzweiflung
desperate [ˈdespərət] verzweifelt
desperately [ˈdespərətlɪ] unbedingt
despite [dɪˈspaɪt] trotz, ungeachtet
developing country [dɪˈveləpɪŋ ˈkʌntrɪ] Entwicklungsland
devote [dɪˈvəʊt] widmen, opfern
dignity [ˈdɪɡnɪtɪ] Würde
dim [dɪm] (halb)dunkel, düster
disabling [dɪˈseɪblɪŋ] körperlichen Schaden verursachend
disadvantaged [ˌdɪsədˈvɑːntɪdʒd] Benachteiligte(r)
disaster [dɪˈzɑːstə] Unglück
discouraged [dɪsˈkʌrɪdʒd] entmutigt
disgust [dɪsˈɡʌst] Ekel, Widerwille
disturbed [dɪˈstɜːbd] gestört, behindert
divorce [dɪˈvɔːs] Scheidung
dodgy [ˈdɒdʒɪ] vertrackt, nicht einwandfrei
domestic [dəˈmestɪk] häuslich, Haus-
dominance [ˈdɒmɪnəns] Vorherrschaft
donor [ˈdəʊnə] Spender(in)
drag [dræɡ] schleppen, schleifen
dragon [ˈdræɡən] Drache
dress up [ˈdresˈʌp] fein anziehen, sich herausputzen
drift [drɪft] getrieben werden
drip [drɪp] (herab)tropfen, -tröpfeln
drown [draʊn] ertrinken
duck [dʌk] sich ducken
dull [dʌl] matt, trübe
dump [dʌmp]: **garbage dump** Müllhalde, Müllabladeplatz
duvet [ˈduːveɪ] Deckbett, Federbett

ease [iːz]: **be at ease** ruhig, entspannt, gelöst sein
easel [ˈiːzl] Staffelei
eaves [iːvz] Dachgesims
ecstatic [ɪkˈstætɪk] verzückt, begeistert, hingerissen
effort [ˈefət] Anstrengung, Bemühung
eliminated [ɪˈlɪmɪneɪtɪd] beseitigt
embarrass [ɪmˈbærəs] lästig sein
embarrassed [ɪmˈbærəst] verlegen, peinlich berührt
enable [ɪnˈeɪbl] befähigen
enamoured (of) [ɪnˈæməd (əv)] sehr angetan (von)
encounter [ɪnˈkaʊntə] begegnen

encouraged [ɪnˈkʌrɪdʒd] ermutigt, ermuntert
endure [ɪnˈdjʊə] ertragen, aushalten
engaged (in) [ɪnˈɡeɪdʒd (ɪn)] beschäftigt (mit)
enslave [ɪnˈsleɪv] versklaven
entire(ly) [ɪnˈtaɪə(lɪ)] völlig, ganz
environment [ɪnˈvaɪərnmənt] Umgebung
envy [ˈenvɪ] beneiden
equipment [ɪˈkwɪpmənt] Ausrüstung
equivalent [ɪˈkwɪvəlnt] gleichwertig, -bedeutend
escort [ɪˈskɔːt] Geleit(schutz) geben
establish o.s. [ɪˈstæblɪʃ] sich etablieren, Geltung verschaffen
esteemed [ɪˈstiːmd] geachtet, geschätzt
event [ɪˈvent] Ereignis
evidence [ˈevɪdəns] Beweis
evil [ˈiːvl] übel, böse
executive [ɪɡˈzekjʊtɪv] leitende(r) Angestellte(r)
exhaustion [ɪɡˈzɔːstʃən] Erschöpfung
expand [ɪkˈspænd] erweitern
expense [ɪkˈspens] Unkosten
exploitation [ˌeksplɔɪˈteɪʃn] Ausnutzung, -beutung
exploitative [ɪkˈsplɔɪtətɪv] ausbeuterisch
exquisite (sense) [ekˈskwɪzɪt] äußerstes, höchstes (Gefühl)
extent [ɪkˈstent]: **to a certain extent** in gewissem Grade; **to what extent** in welchem Umfang
extract [ˈekstrækt] Auszug

face [feɪs] ins Auge sehen
facilities [fəˈsɪlɪtiːz] Einrichtung(en), Anlage(n)
faintly [ˈfeɪntlɪ] schwach, kaum
familiar [fəˈmɪljə]: **be familiar (with)** vertraut, bekannt sein (mit)
fancy [ˈfænsɪ] Phantasie, Einbildungskraft
favour [ˈfeɪvə]: **do a favour** einen Gefallen tun
feature [ˈfiːtʃə] Merkmal, Charakteristikum
fed [fed]: **be fed up (with)** satt haben, die Nase voll haben (von)
fellow [ˈfeləʊ] Gefährte, Gefährtin
fertilisation [ˌfɜːtɪlaɪˈzeɪʃn] Befruchtung
feverish [ˈfiːvərɪʃ] fiebrig
fictional [ˈfɪkʃənl] erfunden
fiddle (with) [ˈfɪdl (wɪð)] herumfuschen (mit)
filthy rich [ˈfɪlθɪ ˈrɪtʃ] stinkreich
finding [ˈfaɪndɪŋ] Erkenntnis, Feststellung
fledged [fledʒd] flügge

flow [fləʊ] Fluss, Strom
focus (on) [ˈfəʊkəs (ɒn)] (sich) konzentrieren, richten (auf)
fond [fɒnd] liebevoll, überaus schön
fortnight [ˈfɔːtnaɪt] vierzehn Tage
funeral [ˈfjuːnərəl] Beerdigung
furious [ˈfjʊərɪəs] wütend
furthermore [ˌfɜːðəˈmɔː] ferner, überdies, außerdem

gain [ɡeɪn] erlangen, erringen
gap [ɡæp] Lücke, Unterbrechung
garbage dump [ˈɡɑːbɪdʒ ˌdʌmp] Müllhalde, Müllabladeplatz
gaze [ɡeɪz] Starren
genius [ˈdʒiːnjəs] Genie
gently [ˈdʒentlɪ] freundlich, milde: **break the news gently to s.o.** jdm. die Nachricht schonend beibringen
genuine [ˈdʒenjʊɪn] aufrichtig
get along (with) [ˌɡet əˈlɒŋ (wɪð)] auskommen (mit)
ghost town [ˈɡəʊst taʊn] Geisterstadt
giggle [ˈɡɪɡl] Gekicher
glance [ɡlɑːns] flüchtiger Blick
glisten [ˈɡlɪsn] glitzern, glänzen
glued (to) [ɡluːd (tə)] wie angewachsen
godchild [ˈɡɒdtʃaɪld] Patenkind
grade [ɡreɪd] einteilen, -stufen
gradual(ly) [ˈɡrædjʊəl(ɪ)] nach und nach
gravel [ˈɡrævl] Kies
grief [ɡriːf] Leid, Schmerz, Gram
grin [ɡrɪn] Grinsen
grip-sack [ˈɡrɪpsæk] Reisetasche
guard [ɡɑːd] Wache, (Wach)posten
guarded [ˈɡɑːdɪd] vorsichtig, zurückhaltend
guilt [ɡɪlt] Schuld

hamlet [ˈhæmlɪt] Weiler, Dörfchen
handle [ˈhændl] umgehen mit, fertig werden,
hard-core pornography [ˌhɑːdkɔːpɔːˈnɒɡrəfɪ] harte Pornografie
hasten [ˈheɪsn] sich beeilen, eilen
hatchery [ˈhætʃərɪ] Brutplatz
haunt [hɔːnt] quälen, verfolgen
hazardous [ˈhæzədəs] gefährlich, riskant
head (for) [ˈhed (fə)] losgehen, -steuern (auf)
heal [hiːl] heilen
heap [hiːp] aufhäufen
heaven [ˈhevn]: **for heaven's sake** um Himmels willen
heels [hiːlz]: **head over heels** kopfüber

hesitate ['hezɪteɪt] zögern
hideaway ['haɪdəweɪ] Zufluchtsort
hideous(ly) ['hɪdɪəs(lɪ)] schrecklich
hinder (from) ['hɪndə (frɒm)] hindern, abhalten (von)
hint [hɪnt] Hinweis, Andeutung
horrid ['hɒrɪd] schrecklich, fürchterlich, entsetzlich
horrify ['hɒrɪfaɪ] entsetzen
host [həʊst] Veranstaltung ausrichten
however poor [haʊˈevə ˈpɔː] wie arm auch (immer)
humble ['hʌmbl] bescheiden

I

idyll ['ɪdɪl] Idylle
ignorance ['ɪgnərəns] Unwissenheit, Unkenntnis
illumination [ɪˌluːmɪˈneɪʃn] Erleuchtung
impact ['ɪmpækt] starker Eindruck
implant ['ɪmplɑːnt] Implantation
impose [ɪmˈpəʊz] auferlegen
imposing [ɪmˈpəʊzɪŋ] eindrucksvoll
impressed (by) [ɪmˈprest (baɪ)] beeindruckt (von)
increase [ɪnˈkriːs] zunehmen, sich vermehren
incredibly [ɪnˈkredɪblɪ] unglaublich
incubator ['ɪŋkjʊˌbeɪtə] Brutkasten
independent [ˌɪndɪˈpendənt] unabhängig
indeterminate [ˌɪndɪˈtɜːmɪnət] unbestimmbar
indicate ['ɪndɪkeɪt] andeuten, (an)zeigen
indiscriminate [ˌɪndɪˈskrɪmɪnət] willkürlich, unkritisch
inevitable [ɪnˈevɪtəbl] unvermeidlich
inhabitant [ɪnˈhæbɪtənt] Bewohner(in)
inseparable [ɪnˈsepərəbl] untrennbar
inspire [ɪnˈspaɪə] inspirieren, beseelen
intelligence [ɪnˈtelɪdʒəns] Nachricht, Mitteilung
intentional(ly) [ɪnˈtenʃənəl(ɪ)] absichtlich
intolerable [ɪnˈtɒlərəbl] unerträglich
invigorate [ɪnˈvɪgəreɪt] stärken, beleben, kräftigen
involved in [ɪnˈvɒlvd ɪn] verwickelt in
irritated ['ɪrɪteɪtɪd] verärgert, irritiert, gereizt
item ['aɪtəm] Gegenstand, Stück

J

jealousy ['dʒeləsɪ] Eifersucht

K

keen [kiːn] begeistert, leidenschaftlich; scharf, durchdringend

keep up (with) [kiːp ˈʌp (wɪð)] sich auf dem Laufenden halten (über)
kneel [niːl] knien
knot [nɒt] Knoten

L

label ['leɪbl] Etikett
labour ['leɪbə] (schwere) Arbeit
lack (of) ['læk (əv)] Mangel (an)
lane [leɪn] (Fahr)Spur
latchkey ['lætʃkiː] Haus-, Wohnungsschlüssel
lawn [lɔːn] Rasen
lay [leɪ]: **what lay in store** was für Überraschungen zu erwarten waren
lecture ['lektʃə] Vortrag, Vorlesung
leisure ['leʒə] Freizeit, Muße
liberate ['lɪbəreɪt] befreien
likely ['laɪklɪ] wahrscheinlich, voraussichtlich
link up (with) [lɪŋk ˈʌp (wɪð)] verbinden (mit)
lobster-red [ˌlɒbstəˈred] krebsrot
long (for) ['lɒŋ (fə)] sich sehnen (nach)
loyalty ['lɔɪəltɪ] Loyalität, Treue

M

magnificent [mægˈnɪfɪsnt] großartig, prächtig, herrlich
marvellous ['mɑːvələs] wunderbar, phantastisch
masterplan ['mɑːstəplæn] Gesamtplan
maternal [məˈtɜːnəl] mütterlich
matter ['mætə]: **in a matter of** innerhalb von
mature [məˈtʃʊə] mündig
megatower ['megəˌtaʊə] (riesen)großer Turm
memory ['memərɪ]: **short-term memory** Kurzzeitgedächtnis
mental ['mentl] geistig, innerlich
mess [mes]: **be in a mess** in der Klemme sein; **look a mess** unordentlich aussehen
mess about [mes əˈbaʊt] sich herumtreiben
minefield ['maɪnfiːld] Minenfeld
misconduct [ˌmɪsˈkɒndʌkt] schlechtes Benehmen
misfit ['mɪsfɪt] Außenseiter(in)
modest ['mɒdɪst] bescheiden
mood [muːd] Stimmung
motionless ['məʊʃnləs] bewegungs-, regungslos
mould [məʊld] formen (nach einem Muster)
moved [muːvd] gerührt, bewegt
muck (about) [ˌmʌk əˈbaʊt] herumlungern
multiply ['mʌltɪplaɪ] vermehren
mutter ['mʌtə] murmeln

N

neat [niːt] sauber, ordentlich
nickname ['nɪkneɪm] Spitzname
nightmare ['naɪtmeə] Alptraum
nod [nɒd] nicken
nursery ['nɜːsərɪ]: **day nursery** Kindertagesstätte, -krippe; **nursery school** Kindergarten
nutrition [njuːˈtrɪʃn] Ernährung, Nahrung

O

obedient [əˈbiːdjənt] gehorsam
object ['ɒbdʒɪkt]: **money is no object** Geld spielt keine Rolle
obligation [ˌɒblɪˈgeɪʃn] Verpflichtung, Verbindlichkeit
obsessed (by) [əbˈsest (baɪ)] besessen (von)
occupant ['ɒkjuːpənt] Bewohner(in), Insasse
occur [əˈkɜː] sich ereignen, vorfallen
offspring ['ɒfsprɪŋ] Nachkommen(schaft)
outburst ['aʊtbɜːst] Ausbruch
outdated [ˌaʊtˈdeɪtɪd] überholt, veraltet
outgrow [aʊtˈgrəʊ] herauswachsen aus

P

pace [peɪs] Geschwindigkeit, Tempo
package tour ['pækɪdʒ ˌtʊə] Pauschalreise
paracetamol [ˌpærəˈsetəmɒl] Schmerzmittel
paralysed ['pærəlaɪzd] gelähmt
part (with) ['pɑːt (wɪð)] sich trennen (von)
participate [pɑːˈtɪsɪpeɪt] teilnehmen
particular(ly) [pəˈtɪkjələ(lɪ)] speziell, besonders
pastime ['pɑːstaɪm] Zeitvertreib
pastry shop ['peɪstrɪ ʃɒp] Konditorei
pasty ['peɪstɪ] käsig, blass (Haut)
pat [pæt] klopfen, tätscheln
patch [pætʃ] Flecken
paternal [pəˈtɜːnəl] väterlich
pattern ['pætn] Muster
peddler (pedlar) ['pedlə] Hausierer
perception [pəˈsepʃn] (geistige) Wahrnehmung
persistence [pəˈsɪstəns] Beharrlichkeit
persuade (o.s.) [pəˈsweɪd] (sich) einreden, überzeugen
pick-up truck ['pɪkʌp ˌtrʌk] offener Last-, Lieferwagen
piercing ['pɪəsɪŋ] durchdringend
pile [paɪl] (auf)schichten

pin [pɪn] (an)heften, -stecken
pitch [pɪtʃ] Stand *(Händler)*
pity ['pɪtɪ] Mitleid haben
plug in(to) ['plʌg ɪn(tə)] einstecken, -stöpseln
plump [plʌmp] plump
pollution [pə'luːʃn] (Umwelt)Verschmutzung
possess [pə'zes] Besitz ergreifen
poverty ['pɒvətɪ] Armut
prayer ['preə] Gebet
pre-recorded [ˌpriːrɪ'kɔːdɪd] bespielt *(Musik/Videokassette)*
preceding [prɪ'siːdɪŋ] vorhergehend
precious ['preʃəs] kostbar, wertvoll
prediction [prɪ'dɪkʃn] Vorhersage
pregnant ['pregnənt] schwanger
pressure ['preʃə] Druck
presumably [prɪ'zuːməblɪ] vermutlich, wahrscheinlich
previous ['priːvɪəs] vorausgehend, vorherig
pride [praɪd]: **burst with pride** platzen vor Stolz; **take pride (in)** stolz sein (auf)
prop up ['prɒp 'ʌp] (ab)stützen
proper(ly) ['prɒpə(lɪ)] richtig, wie es sich gehört
proportion [prə'pɔːʃn] Teil
proposition [prɒpə'zɪʃn] Behauptung
prospect ['prɒspekt] Aussicht, Möglichkeit
prosperity [prɒ'sperɪtɪ] Gedeihen, Glück, Wohlstand
provide [prə'vaɪd] (Gelegenheit) schaffen; zur Verfügung stellen
provided (that) [prə'vaɪdɪd (ðæt)] vorausgesetzt, unter der Bedingung (dass)
puffy ['pʌfɪ] bauschig
punter ['pʌntə] (Glücks)Spieler
puppet ['pʌpɪt] Marionette, Puppe
purr [pɜː] schnurren
pursue [pə'suː] verfolgen, nachgehen
pursuit [pə'suːt] Beschäftigung, Betätigung
pushchair ['pʊʃtʃeə] (Kinder)Sportwagen
put [pʊt]: **put down** demütigen, heruntersetzen; **put up** einen Gast (bei sich) aufnehmen
puzzled ['pʌzld] vor einem Rätsel stehen

R

raffle ['ræfl] Tombola, Verlosung
rag [ræg] Fetzen, Lumpen
random ['rændəm]: **at random** aufs Geratewohl, blindlings
rank [ræŋk] Rang
rat race ['ræt reɪs] harter (Konkurrenz)Kampf
readership ['riːdəʃɪp] Leserschaft
reckon ['rekn] der Meinung sein

recommendation [ˌrekəmen'deɪʃn] Empfehlung
recover [rɪ'kʌvə] (Gesundheit) wiedererlangen
reduce [rɪ'djuːs] vermindern, -ringern
reduction [rɪ'dʌkʃn]: **weight reduction** Gewichtsabnahme
reflect [rɪ'flekt] widerspiegeln, zeigen; nachdenken, überlegen
refuge ['refjuːdʒ] Schutz, Zufluchtsort
regain [rɪ'geɪn] wiedergewinnen
relationship [rɪ'leɪʃnʃɪp] Beziehung, Verhältnis
relatively ['relətɪvlɪ] verhältnismäßig
release [rɪ'liːs] freisetzen, auslösen
relief [rɪ'liːf] Erleichterung
remain [rɪ'meɪn] (bestehen) bleiben
repression [rɪ'preʃn] Unterdrückung, Verdrängung
require [rɪ'kwaɪə] erfordern
rescue ['reskjuː] retten
research [rɪ'sɜːtʃ] Forschung(sarbeit)
reservations [rezə'veɪʃnz] Vorbehalt
resplendent [rɪ'splendənt] glänzend, strahlend
restless ['restləs] ruhe-, rastlos
restored [rɪ'stɔːd] restauriert, in Stand gesetzt
retailer ['riːteɪlə] Einzelhändler
retirement [rɪ'taɪəmənt] Ruhestand
return [rɪ'tɜːn]: **in return** als Gegenleistung
reunion [ˌriː'juːnjən] Wiedervereinigung
reveal [rɪ'viːl] zeigen, erkennen lassen
reverse [rɪ'vɜːs] in die entgegengesetzte Richtung bringen
revision [rɪ'vɪʒn] Überarbeitung, Wiederholung
revitalise [rɪ'vaɪtəlaɪz] neu beleben
reward [rɪ'wɔːd] belohnen
rewarding [rɪ'wɔːdɪŋ] lohnend, dankbar *(Aufgabe)*
ridiculous [rɪ'dɪkjələs] lächerlich
rights [raɪts]: **human rights** Menschenrechte
riot ['raɪət]: **run riot** durchgehen *(Phantasie)*
ripe [raɪp] reif, gereift
roadsweeper ['rəʊdswiːpə] Straßenfeger, -kehrer
roam [rəʊm] umherstreifen
rough [rʌf] rauh, zerklüftet
roving ['rəʊvɪŋ] umherziehend, -streifend
row [raʊ] Krach, Streit
rubber cape ['rʌbə keɪp] Gummiumhang
rural ['rʊərəl] ländlich

S

sake [seɪk]: **for heaven's sake** um Himmels willen; **for the sake (of)** um ... willen

sample ['saːmpl] (aus)probieren
save [seɪv] außer
scared ['skeəd]: **be scared (of)** sich fürchten (vor); **scared stiff** zu Tode erschrocken
scary ['skeərɪ] gruselig, unheimlich
scents [sents] Geruch, Duft
sceptical ['skeptɪkl] skeptisch, misstrauisch
scheme [skiːm] Projekt, Programm
scold [skəʊld] (aus)schimpfen
score [skɔː] Punkte erzielen
security [sɪ'kjʊərətɪ] Sicherheit: **social security** Sozialhilfe
seed [siːd] Samen
seek out ['siːk 'aʊt] herausfinden, aufspüren
selectively [sɪ'lektɪvlɪ] auswählend, durch Auswahl
self-assertion [ˌselfə'sɜːʃn] Selbstbehauptung
self-esteem [ˌselfɪ'stiːm] Selbstachtung
self-image [ˌself'ɪmɪdʒ] Selbstverständnis
self-supporting [ˌselfsə'pɔːtɪŋ] selbstversorgend
self-worth [ˌself'wɜːθ] Selbstwert
selfishness ['selfɪʃnəs] Selbstsucht, Egoismus
sense (of) ['sens əv] Sinn, Empfindung, Gefühl (für)
sense [sens] fühlen, spüren
sentence ['sentəns]: **death sentence** Todesurteil, -strafe
servant ['sɜːvənt] Diener(in)
set up ['set 'ʌp] errichten
shape [ʃeɪp]: **in shape** in Form
share [ʃeə] Geschäftsanteil, Kapitalanlage
sharp [ʃɑːp] gescheit, aufgeweckt
shelter ['ʃeltə] Zuflucht, Schutz geben
shift [ʃɪft] die Lage wechseln, sich bewegen
short-term memory ['ʃɔːt ˌtɜːm ˌmemərɪ] Kurzzeitgedächtnis
show-off ['ʃəʊɒf] Angeber, Protzer
shrug [ʃrʌg] die Achseln zucken
shudder ['ʃʌdə] Schauder(n)
sigh [saɪ] Seufzer
significance [sɪg'nɪfɪkəns] Bedeutung, Wichtigkeit
significant(ly) [sɪg'nɪfɪkənt(lɪ)] merklich
silk [sɪlk] Seide
simultaneous(ly) [sɪməl'teɪnɪəs(lɪ)] gleichzeitig
sip [sɪp] nippen, schlürfen
skill [skɪl] Geschick(lichkeit), Können
skyscraper ['skaɪskreɪpə] Wolkenkratzer
slash [slæʃ] Schnitt(wunde)
slave [sleɪv] Sklave, Sklavin
slender ['slendə] schlank, schmal

slight idea ['slaɪt aɪ'dɪə] schwache, geringe Vorstellung

sloppy speech ['slɒpɪ 'spiːtʃ] saloppe Sprache

smart [smɑːt] schick, modisch

smashed [smæʃd] besoffen, 'blau'

snatch [snætʃ] schnappen, packen

sob [sɒb] Schluchzen

sober ['səʊbə] nüchtern

sociable ['səʊʃəbl] gesellig, umgänglich

socialise ['səʊʃəlaɪz] unter die Leute gehen

solve [sɒlv] lösen, klären

sophisticated [sə'fɪstɪkeɪtɪd] weltklug, intellektuell

soul [səʊl] Seele

source [sɔːs] Quelle, Ursprung

sparkling ['spɑːklɪŋ] funkelnd, sprühend

sparrow ['spærəʊ] Spatz

specific [spə'sɪfɪk] speziell, bestimmt

spectacular [spek'tækjʊlə] Aufsehen erregend, sensationell

spit [spɪt] spucken

split [splɪt] (sich) teilen

spot [spɒt]: **on the spot** auf der Stelle, sofort

spot [spɒt] entdecken, erspähen

square [skweə] Spießer

stable ['steɪbl] sicher, dauerhaft

stand (for) ['stænd (fə)] stehen (für), bedeuten

stare [steə]: **vacant stare** geistloser Blick

stare [steə] anstarren, große Augen machen

startling ['stɑːtlɪŋ] verblüffend, Aufsehen erregend

steel [stiːl] Stahl

stifling ['staɪflɪŋ] erstickend, stickig

stirred [stɜːd] aufgewühlt, bewegt, erregt

storage ['stɔːrɪdʒ] (Ein)Lagerung, Lager

store [stɔː]: **what lay in store** was für Überraschungen zu erwarten waren

storey (story) ['stɔːrɪ] Stockwerk

strike [straɪk] beeindrucken, auffallen

strive [straɪv] sich bemühen

stroke [strəʊk] (Herz)Schlag

stroke [strəʊk] streichen über, streicheln

struggle ['strʌgl] kämpfen, ringen

strut [strʌt] stolzieren

stuff [stʌf] Zeug, Sachen

subtle ['sʌtl] fein, subtil

suburb ['sʌbɜːb] Vorstadt, -ort

sufficiently [sə'fɪʃəntlɪ] genügend, ausreichend

suicide ['sʊɪsaɪd] Selbstmord

sulk [sʌlk] schmollen

supply [sə'plaɪ] liefern, (Nachfrage) decken

supposing [sə'pəʊzɪŋ] angenommen

supreme [sʊ'priːm] höchst, äußerst

surface ['sɜːfɪs] auftauchen

surge [sɜːdʒ] Aufwallung, Woge (der Gefühle)

survey ['sɜːveɪ] Umfrage

survival [sə'vaɪvl] Überleben

suspension [sə'spenʃn] Abwesenheit

switch on [ˌswɪtʃ 'ɒn] einschalten

T

temper ['tempə] Laune, Stimmung

tempted ['temptɪd]: **feel/be tempted** versucht, geneigt sein

tempting ['temptɪŋ] verführerisch, verlockend

tend (to) ['tend (tə)] tendieren, neigen (zu)

tender ['tendə] zart

tension ['tenʃn] Spannung

terms [tɜːmz]: **in general terms** allgemein ausgedrückt

terrified ['terɪfaɪd] erschrocken, verängstigt, entsetzt

thoroughly ['θʌrəlɪ] gründlich, eingehend

tick [tɪk] abhaken *(Liste)*

tie down ['taɪ 'daʊn] festbinden

token ['təʊkən] Spielmarke

tot [tɒt] Knirps, Kerlchen

tough [tʌf] hartnäckig

track [træk]: **off the beaten track** abgelegen

trading ['treɪdɪŋ] Handel

trainers ['treɪnəz] Turnschuhe

transfer (to) [træns'fɜː (tə)] versetzen (nach)

travel-stained ['trævlˌsteɪnd] von der Reise beschmutzt

tremble ['trembl] zittern

trot [trɒt] trotten

truck [trʌk]: **pick-up truck** offener Last-, Lieferwagen

truly ['truːlɪ] aufrichtig

trunks [trʌŋks]: **swimming trunks** Badehose

tube [tjuːb] (Glas)Röhrchen

tumultuous(ly) [tjuː'mʌltjʊəs(lɪ)] heftig, stürmisch

tune [tjuːn] in Schwung bringen

twins [twɪnz] Zwillinge

twitter ['twɪtə] zwitschern

U

undergo [ˌʌndə'gəʊ] durchmachen

universal(ly) [juːnɪ'vɜːsəl(ɪ)] allgemein

unjustifiable [ʌnˌdʒʌstɪ'faɪəbl] unverantwortlich, nicht zu rechtfertigen(d)

unlikely [ʌn'laɪklɪ] unwahrscheinlich

unwitting(ly) [ʌn'wɪtɪŋ(lɪ)] unabsichtlich, unwissentlich

upsetting [ʌp'setɪŋ] bestürzend

upside down ['ʌpsaɪd ˌdaʊn] auf den Kopf gestellt

urgent(ly) ['ɜːdʒnt(lɪ)] dringend

utter ['ʌtə] aussprechen, äußern

utterly ['ʌtəlɪ] äußerst, höchst, völlig

V

vacant stare ['veɪknt 'steə] geistloser Blick

vast [vɑːst] (riesen)groß, gewaltig

vastness ['vɑːstnəs] Weite, Unermesslichkeit

vessel ['vesl]: **blood vessel** (Blut)Gefäß

victim ['vɪktɪm] Opfer, (Unfall)Tote(r)

vigorous(ly) ['vɪgərəs(lɪ)] kräftig, nachdrücklich

violence ['vaɪələns] Gewalt(tätigkeit)

virtually ['vɜːtjʊəlɪ] eigentlich, im Grunde (genommen)

virtue ['vɜːtjuː] Tugend(haftigkeit)

vocal coded ['vəʊkl 'kəʊdɪd] (auf Band) gesprochen

W

waste [weɪst]: **nuclear waste** Atommüll

wave one's hand ['weɪv wʌnz 'hænd] mit der Hand winken

wed [wed] ehelichen, heiraten

weedy ['wiːdɪ] unkrautartig

weep [wiːp] weinen

weight reduction ['weɪt rɪ'dʌkʃn] Gewichtsabnahme

weird ['wiːəd] ulkig, verrückt

welfare ['welfeə] Wohlergehen

well-off [ˌwel'ɒf] wohlhabend, gutsituiert

wheel [wiːl] sich bewegen, rollen

wheelchair ['wiːltʃeə] Rollstuhl

whereas [weər'æz] während, wohingegen

whisper ['wɪspə] flüstern

whitewash ['waɪtwɒʃ] reinwaschen, rehabilitieren

widow ['wɪdəʊ] Witwe

witness ['wɪtnəs] Zeuge, Zeugin

wrapped up ['ræpt ʌp] eingepackt

wretch [retʃ] Tropf, Wesen

wrinkle ['rɪŋkl] Runzel, Falte

X

X-rays ['eksreɪz] Röntgenstrahlen

Y

yell [jel] schreien, brüllen

Acknowledgements

Photographs

We are grateful to the following for permission to reproduce copyright material:

Cover photographs: Bildarchiv Mauritius, Mittenwald (bottom by C. Bayer), Amos Schliack, Hamburg (background)

Beate Andler-Teufel, München: page 20 (background), 31 (no 1), 35 (left)
Australian Embassy, Bonn: page 46 (top)
Bavaria Bildagentur GmbH, Gauting b. München: page 16 (no 3), 19 (no 4, 5, 6), 31 (no 2, 4)
John Birdsall, Nottingham: page 32 , 56 (left) (top)
Gareth Boden, Hertford: page 8 (bottom right) (top left), 34 (no 1, 2, 3)
Hugo Boss AG, Metzingen: page 23
Comstock Fotoagentur, Berlin: page 37 (no 4)
Corbis UK Ltd., London: page 35 (right)
Corel Stock Photo Library: page 9 (background), 25 (no 1, 2, 4), 28 (middle left), 31 (middle right) (1st from bottom right), 46 (middle right), 47
Graeme Cunningham, Beckenham: page 7 (no 4)
Escada, Aschheim: page 7 (no 2 by Guy Marineau)
Mary Evans Picture Library, London: page 39 (bottom)
Focus GmbH, Hamburg: page 20 (left by Mehau Kulyk/Science Photo Library)
Lydia Glaubitz, München: page 26 (right), 37 (no 1)
Sally and Richard Greenhill, London: page 7 (no 1), 9, 10 (no 3), 15
IFA Bilderteam GmbH, München: page 18 (by Bumann)
The Image Bank Bildagentur, München: page 7 (no 3 by William Sallaz), 19 (no 3 by Chris M. Rogers), 33, 36 (left by Ulf Wallin)
Interfoto Pressebild-Agentur Bildarchiv, München: page 31 (2nd from top right) (2nd from bottom right) (1st from top)
Langenscheidt-Longman Archiv, München: page 13 (no 4), 39 (top)
Bettina Lindenberg, München: page 36 (right)
Otto Versand, Hamburg: page 22
Oxford University Press, New York: page 37 (no 5 by Lemoyne), 40 (by Edinger), 41 (left by Vauclair)

PA News, London: page 13 (no 3), 30 (by David Jones)
Premium Stock Photography GmbH, Düsseldorf: page 26 (left by A. Rossi), 42
Claudia Schwarz, München: page 24
Silvia Stephan, Offenburg: page 8 (top right) (bottom middle) (bottom left),10 (no 1, 2), 13 (no 1),19 (no 1, 2), 20 (right), 25 (no 3), 27, 28 (middle right) (bottom right) (top), 29, 37 (no 6, 3), 38, 41 (right), 48
Tony Stone Bilderwelten, München: page 21 (by Tim Davies)
Superbild Bildarchiv Erich Bach, Grünwald: page 53 (by Bernd Ducke)
Transglobe Agency, Hamburg: page 13 (no 2)
John Walmsley, Guildford: page 12, 14, 16 (no 1, 2), 28 (bottom left), 37 (no 2)
Zefa Zentrale Farbbild Agentur GmbH, Düsseldorf: page 46 (bottom) (middle left by Janicek)

Illustrations

Philip Bannister, Pershore: page 55, 56, 57, 58, 59
Debbie Hinks, Brighton: page 43, 44, 48, 49, 50
Julian Page, South Croydon: page 51, 52
Chris Ryley, Tangmere: page 12, 36, 60, 61, 63, 64, 65, 66, 67, 68, 69, 70, 71

Texts

We would like to thank the following for their kind permission to use articles, extracts or adaptations from copyright material:

Caroline Scott/The Sunday Times, London: page 9;
Times Educational Supplement, London: page 15;
Independent Newspapers Ltd., London: page 17;
Jonathan Miller/Times Newspapers Ltd. 1994, London: page 27;
Guardian Newspapers Ltd., London: page 39; 56
Random House UK Ltd., London: page 43;
Penguin Books Australia Ltd.; Ringwood, Vic.: page 47
Millie Peters/Times Newspapers Ltd. 1994, London: page 51
Chatto and Windus, London: page 53

We should be grateful for any information which might assist us in tracing the copyright owners of sources which we have been unable to acknowledge.

*Wir führen auch die bekannten **Penguin Readers** in unserem Programm. Mit den folgenden Lektüren, die auf Ihre Lernstufe abgestimmt sind, können Sie Unterhaltsames und Spannendes in der Originalsprache lesen und so »ganz nebenbei« Ihren Wortschatz erweitern und Ihr Englisch verbessern.*

The Chamber
John Grisham
Sam Cayhall wartet seit Jahren in der Todeszelle auf seine Hinrichtung. Der junge Anwalt Adam Hall möchte einen weiteren Aufschub der Urteilsvollstreckung erreichen. Sam möchte nichts mit ihm zu tun haben – doch Adam kennt ein Geheimnis, mit dem er Einfluss auf den alten Mann nehmen kann…
Bestellnr. 3-526-**36 411**-7

The Grass is Singing
Doris Lessing
Die weiße südafrikanische Farmersfrau Mary ist unglücklich in ihrer Ehe. Für ihren schwarzen Hausboy hegt sie leidenschaftliche Gefühle, doch sie behandelt ihn, wie sie alle Schwarzen behandelt: sehr grausam…
Bestellnr. 3-526-**41 789**-X

Misery
Stephen King
Nach einem Autounfall hält Anni Wilkes den Schriftsteller Paul Sheldon in ihrem Haus gefangen. Die geistig verwirrte Krankenschwester will verhindern, dass der Autor die von ihr so geliebte Romanfigur Misery Chastain sterben lässt.
Bestellnr. 3-526-**41 829**-2

Presumed Innocent
Scott Turow
In New York wird eine ehrgeizige Anwältin ermordet. Bei seinen Ermittlungen kämpft Rusty Sabich, der auch ihr Geliebter war, um seinen guten Ruf, seine Ehe und sein Leben.
Bestellnr. 3-526-**41 795**-4

The Rainmaker
John Grisham
In seinem ersten Fall vor Gericht tritt Anwalt Rudy Baylor gegen einen übermächtigen Versicherungskonzern an, der sich weigert, den Eltern eines leukämiekranken jungen Mannes das Geld für die lebensrettende Therapie zu zahlen.
Bestellnr. 3-526-**36 412**-5

A Time to Kill
John Grisham
Der Farbige Lee Hailey erschießt zwei weiße Männer, die seine 10-jährige Tochter vergewaltigt haben. In einem Klima von Zorn und Gewalt wird es gefährlich für den jungen Anwalt Jake Brigance; doch er ist fest entschlossen, seinen Mandanten und sein eigenes Leben zu verteidigen.
Bestellnr. 3-526-**36 410** 0

Fragen Sie Ihren Buchhändler nach diesen Titeln – oder bestellen Sie mit der Bestellkarte beim Verlag.

Ich bestelle hiermit die folgenden Lektüren:

○ **The Chamber**
(Best.-Nr. 3-526-**36 411**-7 / € 7,10 [D] / € 7,30 [A] / sFr. 13,70)

○ **The Grass is Singing**
(Best.-Nr. 3-526-**41 789**-X / € 6,65 [D] / € 6,90 [A] / sFr. 13,20)

○ **Misery**
(Best.-Nr. 3-526-**41 829**-2 / € 7,05 [D] / € 7,30 [A] / sFr. 13,70)

○ **Presumed Innocent**
(Best.-Nr. 3-526-**41 795**-4 / € 7,05 [D] / € 7,30 [A] / sFr. 13,70)

○ **The Rainmaker**
(Best.-Nr. 3-526-**36 412**-5 / € 6,65 [D] / € 6,90 [A] / sFr. 13,20)

○ **A Time to Kill**
(Best.-Nr. 3-526-**36 410**-9 / € 6,65 [D] / € 6,90 [A] / sFr. 13,20)

Preisänderungen vorbehalten

- Zutreffendes ist angekreuzt -

Unterschrift/Datum

(Absender auf Vorderseite ----->)

Absender:

_____

Name/Vorname

_____

Straße/Nr.

_____

PLZ/Ort

Bitte liefern Sie die angekreuzten Titel
über die Buchhandlung:

_____

Name/Straße

_____

PLZ/Ort

*(Sollte keine Buchhandlung genannt sein,
erfolgt die Lieferung über eine Buchhandlung nach Wahl des Verlags.)*

Antwort

**An den Verlag
Langenscheidt-Longman
Postfach 40 11 20**

80711 München